Being N(
In Clapham Junction

Unveiling the Path to Inner Peace and Happiness

MOICH ABRAHAMS

WOW Book Publishing™

Copyright

First Edition Published by Moich Abrahams Copyright

@ 2023 Moich Abrahams

Published by: WOW Book Publishing™

Printed by: Amazon.com

All rights reserved. This book is protected by copyright. No part of this publication may be sold or reproduced in any form without permission in writing from the author. No part of this book may be reproduced in any form or by any electronic or mechanical means, including information storage and retrieval systems, without permission in writing from the author. The only exception is by a reviewer, who may quote short excerpts in a review.

The purpose of this book is to provide education and entertainment. The views and opinions expressed in this book are those of the author, based on his personal experiences and education. The author shall neither be liable nor responsible for any loss or damage allegedly arising from any information or suggestion in this book. The author does not guarantee that anyone following the techniques, suggestions, ideas or strategies will become successful. The author and publisher take no responsibility for what you may experience as a result of following some of the ideas or practices mentioned.

The author retains the right under the Copyright, Design and Patent Act, 1988, to be identified as the author of this work. "

Dedication

I dedicate this book with much love to my friend Michael to celebrate his uniqueness in his spiritual approach to life, and to you as you discover the power of peace and happiness.

*– **Moich Abrahams***

Foreword

I know what a challenge and achievement it is to write and publish one's first book. As an Award-Winning Author, International Speaker, and Publisher, I can only heap praise on this first-time author. Moich has chosen to write about a fascinating character and the extraordinary philosophy which they have in common.

I completely agree that getting to know oneself in the fullest way possible is essential to have as a basis for doing great things in life. The philosophy that Moich alludes to as key to understanding his friend Michael's life, absolutely goes into this in a most profound way. It's as transforming and life enhancing as any enquiry could be. Moich Abrahams has written with sensitivity and passion about this especially in connection with the story of lifelong practitioner, Michael Bruce Proudfoot.

Reading this book, you will experience Moich's amazing creativity, imagination and empathy for a very unusual man. I think Moich has done an excellent job of exploring in the widest context, Michael's route from having had a very privileged and one might say illustrious background to becoming a modern-day mystic.

An important quality that Moich possesses is a rare insight into the psychology of people who suffer from emotional and behavioural issues; indeed, his working career was as an Advisor in Special Educational Needs and he has a huge compassion and understanding in this regard. He is very intuitive, perceptive and immensely caring and this book will introduce you to a fascinating spiritual characteralong with insights rare to find.

If you are interested in spiritual development, especially from the perspective of Non-Duality, and getting to know yourself at a deep level, or just prepared to explore appreciating human beings, as the saying goes, to not mistake the book cover for the content, then this book will provide an interesting read for you. I commend it whole heartedly and hope you enjoy it.

Vishal Morjaria –
Award-Winning Author,
International Speaker and Publisher

Testimonials

"I have known Moich for 23 years. He is one of the most magical, creative, playful, imaginative people I have met in my entire life. The aliveness, curiosity and magical thinking has been a source of delight and joy in my life. Moich had a significant impact on the direction of my life for which I will always be grateful. Enjoy reading this book and allow its deeper message to reach your heart."

**Gosia Gorna,
International Speaker, Bestselling Author of 'The Expansion Game', Transformational Coach and Intuitive,
London**

"I have known Moich for the last 18 years. We used to meet every time he came to Malta and participated in one of my spiritual seminars. Moich has always impressed me with the combination and flow of many of his attributes and gifts, namely silence, great attentiveness, extreme focus and precision in his interventions and questions.

This comes out very powerfully in the way Moich cultivated the friendship with Michael and manages to 'read' his soul and bring out the beauty of his personality and beliefs."

**Godwin Genovese,
A professional Social Worker in Malta - teaching spirituality for the past 40 years
(https://quietopenness.blogspot.com/)**

"Moich writes tenderly about his friendship with Michael, how it started and then grew. Moich gradually unearths the amazing story of a man that most people would dismiss and walk past. He illuminates the essence of Michael for us beautifully and reminds us to look beyond appearances and our own judgments to see the humanity within everyone. Thank you, Moich. Thank you, Michael."

**Nick Williams,
Leadership Guide and Author of eighteen books including, 'The Work We Were Born to Do'**

"A beautifully written account of Moich's friendship with Michael and how their shared awareness of our true nature brought them together. It's a reminder to us all that present moment awareness is all there ever is. Many people today are exploring Non-Duality teachings and the Direct Path. This book is a welcome and refreshing account of this exploration in everyday life. Moich is very perceptive and writes with sensitivity and compassion."

**Neil French,
Clinical Psychologist (www.thepowerofnow.co.uk)**

"I love the book, many of us stand and judge people when they seem to be different, I find it commendable that Moich has built such a great friendship with Michael and I believe this book holds many life lessons."

**Pauline Barath,
Author and Book Angel**

"Life presents us all with unexpected teachers and guides that seem for some reason to arrive at just the right time in our lives. Such is the case with Michael in this book whose outer demeanour speaks of poverty and deprivation but whose inner core reveals unexpected riches and deep roots. Moich writes compassionately about the evolution of his relationship with this 'urban guru' and how he makes such a deep impression on him from the moment they meet in a cafe near Clapham Junction.

The development of their friendship and the revelations from their conversations are heart-warming, showing how the intimate interaction between two people can help to lift the veil of separation and loneliness and reveal a greater field of love and awareness from apparently unpromising beginnings."

**Philip Marvin –
He has for over forty years been a Non-Duality teacher. He has also run Shakespeare courses and retreats delvinginto the different levels of meaning hidden in Shakespeare's works. He worked for many years as a journalist for Reuters, The Financial Times and as a freelancer**

"An original, passionate and sensitive piece of storytelling, with a great message."

**Malcolm Stern,
Co-founder of Alternatives, psychotherapistand author of 'Slay your Dragons with Compassion'**

"Moich is into Art and Spirituality and I got to know him through related meetings in Malta. Consciousness was a common topic. His book explores Michael's rich cultural and spiritual journey and also the profound topic of Non-Duality.

It will certainly captivate and enlighten readers. Moich's background of working in Special Educational Needs and his workshops on Intuition allows him to relate intimately to Michael's complex personality."

**Mary Attard,
Writer, Photographer and Author of a photographic book titled Contemplation.
She manages a Blog on spiritual/psychological topics called Quiet Openness**

"With just a few pen strokes, Moich makes his subject Michael jump off the page, leaving us eagerly wanting to know more about this fascinating character and his odd lifestyle. We also get to learn as much about Moich's natural empathy as we do about his subject."

**Yanky Fachler,
Broadcaster, Copywriter, Historian, Public Speaker, and Author of seventeen books including '6 Officers, 2 Lions and 750 Mules'**

"Every day we pass seemingly unremarkable people without stopping to get to know them or even talk to them. Moich Abrahams does stop and here tells the fascinating story of his friendship with one of those people - Michael - who, at 90, reveals the details of a fascinating life. This book will reward you with the pleasure of also meeting Michael - and Moich."

**Jurgen Wolff,
International Writing Coach and the Author of the book
'Creativity Now!' (Pearson)**

Acknowledgements

Enormous gratitude to my friend Mary Attard of Malta, who is awesomely skilled at everything to do with book production and authorship and for giving me freely so much of her time and energy, contributing hugely with copy editing and editorial suggestions.

Also, many thanks to Rob Wilkinson living in Scotland who gave me a kick-start reviewing a couple of chapters towards the end of the book and a special thanks to Pauline Barath and Colette Mostert, both real angels, for helping me to keep on track with this book project.

Luckily, I was most fortunate to have the above support because we now live in an age where we are able to communicate over vast distances using the internet and in particular, Zoom. Most of the photographs were taken by Moich Abrahams, and the three little sketches (pages 31, 37, 44) of Michael's father, stepmother, and a young Michael were also made by him.

It goes without saying that I am most gratefully indebted to Michael who was so inspiring and patiently put up with all my questions.

About the Author

Moich Abrahams was born into a Jewish émigré family (to a Hungarian mother and a father of Belarussian descent) and grew up in Letchworth Garden City, in Hertfordshire. He read Maths at King's College London, then taught maths and drawing to children with special needs, specialising in supporting those who had emotional, behavioural and learning difficulties. He then decided to become an artist and trained at Byam Shaw School of Art, now St Martins (1970-73). Afterwards he continued to teach
Special Education before studying for an MA (Fine Art) at Goldsmiths (1980-82).

Moich says he was an academic late developer which provided him with a keen appreciation of people who were a bit different from the norm. He also has a great intuition and ran highly successful workshops, in the 80s through to the naughties, initially teaching everything to do with psychic abilities, later focussing on training people to develop their intuition as a skill.

Moich's artwork is expressive and imaginative and informed by his ongoing interest in "Outsider Art" (Art Brut). To see his art works visit www.moichcreations.com

 He enjoys combining spontaneity and playfulness with exploring deeper aspects of the unconscious, and is fascinated with both unwrapping the mysterious and reinventing child-like expressiveness. Central to this process is the art of "letting go".

He currently describes his work as 'Post-Expressionist Neo-Dada' though it is so unique it is hard to categorise. If you like Picasso, Miro and Basquiat, you will like Moich's work too as he thinks in the same way. Currently Moich is working on creating a new website to replace his older art website (www.moichabrahams.co.uk). For latest developments of this go to www.moichcreations.com. Moich also has an unusual virtual exhibition in a 'gallery on the moon'. This is a non-terrestrial first. (https://curat10n.com/moich-moon)

Moich has studied many spiritual philosophies in depth over his long life, from Kabbalah to Buddhism, Zen and Tantra through to Spiritualism, and Mysticism from all ages.

He now says with great enthusiasm and joy that, at last he has found the path that makes the most sense to him; one which he says gives the fastest route to discovering inner peace. This is via the study of 'Non-Duality' along with the so called 'enquiry' into 'Who am I?' sometimes called "The Direct Path". All this has given Moich a perfect background for taking on the challenging prospect of writing a homily for his friend Michael.

Prologue

Moich Abrahams, March 2021

This book attempts to explore the life and psyche of my dear friend Michael Bruce Proudfoot. Whilst researching for his biography I found him more profound than one may think and since we both share an interest in 'Self-Enquiry', I was impelled in sharing his philosophy in some depth here.

Nonetheless, it must be pointed out from the start that this book may not be quite an accurate portrayal of events regarding Michael's life. Any errors or misrepresentations must be on my head; situations described were often assessed from my limited viewpoint. There are several overlaps and repetitions for which I apologise as I attempt to weaved the threads of Michael's life together. It was also quite a challenge to extract information from him being a very reclusive fellow. Facts were given in a somewhat fragmented and vague way, many times gleaned from rambling remarks, leaving gaps in the jigsaw puzzle of his life.

I must admit that, as you'll come to observe, I've frequently chronicled these 'gleanings' in much the same disconnected fashion as I received them. Additionally, you might notice that I haven't always made a clear distinction between reporting Michael's words and recounting the tale myself, or employing the appropriate quotation marks.

Occasionally, the narrative has also shifted between the present and past tenses. I hope you'll graciously and generously allow for a certain flexibility in your interpretation of the text, considering these factors. Much of the research took place during the Covid Pandemic circa 2019-21 which is occasionally referred to in this book.

Regarding my humble efforts, whilst aspiring to be as accurate as was possible in the circumstances, this needs to be said: I tend to allude to the notion that what we refer to as 'reality' is considered in some way as an illusion for the Self-Realised' (whatever that means). In this light it may be wise to contemplate this account with a bit of poetic licence perhaps as if being narrated by a 'dreamer'.

Concerning the back story of this book, the mastery of peace and happiness, it could be appreciated best by those who are acquainted with the investigation referred to as 'Self-Enquiry', and particularly when familiar with Non- Duality teachings.

Such pursuits are not easy matters to explore and can prove challenging to one's ego. There is a route referred to as The Direct Path, which the author recommends as being the key to opening the door to this topic.

You will find a link to ample material and resources about this at the end of the book.

TABLE OF CONTENTS

CHAPTER 1 - THE LIFE STORY OF MICHAEL PROUDFOOT	9
CHAPTER 2 - ANCESTRY	21
CHAPTER 3 - MICHAEL'S MOTHER	25
CHAPTER 4 - MICHAEL'S FATHER	31
CHAPTER 5 - MICHAEL'S STEPMOTHER	37
CHAPTER 6 - SCHOOLS	43
CHAPTER 7 - LIFE IN CHELSEA	57
CHAPTER 8 - PARIS	73
CHAPTER 9 - LONDON IN THE 50'S	87
CHAPTER 10 - COLET HOUSE	99
CHAPTER 11 - SPIRITUAL CRISIS & REALISATION	113
CHAPTER 12 - BECOMING AN URBAN HERMIT	137
CHAPTER 13 - PHOTOS OF MICHAEL	147
CHAPTER 14 - FRIENDS & HANGOUTS	155
CHAPTER 15 - SONGS & LITERATURE	169
CHAPTER 16 - SATSANG WITH MICHAEL	189
CHAPTER 17 - THE THREE M'S	213

CHAPTER 1

The life story of Michael Bruce Proudfoot

> *"Biographies are but the clothes and buttons of the man. The biography of the man himself cannot be written"*
>
> **Mark Twain**

I first met Michael sometime in the mid-1980s, when I used to go for my lunch to a small cafe, appropriately named 'Piggies' - because the portions served are always so ample, in Falcon Road, in London, a busy road opposite the side entrance to Clapham Junction Railway Station.

This area, at most times, is full of people shopping or jumping on or off the buses at the many nearby bus stops or in transit via the railway station. It is certainly one of the busiest stations in Europe.

Piggies is a popular workman's cafe restaurant run by a very nice Portuguese man called Joe. He has a shiny round face with well-groomed dark, wavy black hair. With his large white apron tied neatly up behind his

CHAPTER 1 - THE LIFE STORY OF MICHAEL PROUDFOOT

back, he gave the impression of the perfect chef. His cafe was often full of Portuguese people all chatting away in their native tongue.

As was obvious from the framed photos of his favourite Portuguese football teams which crammed the wall space, Joe was a passionate supporter of football. I liked going there because Joe always had a friendly word for me, not only because I was a regular customer but because I was not the usual workman type of client who normally frequented the place. I usually engaged with him with a bit of intelligent conversation whilst ordering my meal, which he liked.

At that time, as I am now, I was very involved with Art, making paintings and prints and having exhibitions. To get a feel for that visit www.moichcreations.com or, if the new website is not yet up and running, you are welcome to visit **www.moichabrahams.co.uk**

As a financial backup, in those days, I worked as a teacher in two local primary schools, one Catholic and one Church of England, just around the corner from Piggies Cafe. My job description was that of a Special Needs Advisor. In spite of this slightly imposing title, though referring to various advisory responsibilities that I had, my main job was actually hands-on teaching children who were deemed by the schools as needing special attention.

Specifically, my role was to support children with

emotional and behavioural issues who would also have learning problems. I believe the current politically correct 'label' may be stated as children who have an emotional or learning 'disability'. I think the term special needs may be out of favour although back then, in the 1980s and earlier, the term 'special needs' was used.

My interest in this work probably originated from the fact that, as a child, I was a 'late developer' myself. Also, because of my long professional experience working with children who were a bit different from the average child, I was able to relate to and recognise signs of similar emotional dissonance in an older youth or an adult. I remember well that day when I first met Michael. I had come to Piggies on a rather wet miserable winter's day where the cold was just bearable, for my lunch break. I was really hungry.

Joe always fixed me a great warm meal which at that time in my life tended to include more meat than I eat these days. I chose liver and mash with boiled cabbage from Piggie's generous daily menu. After a few pleasantries exchanged with Joe whilst ordering my food, I noticed an odd sort of fellow sitting in the corner. Somehow, he seemed to be a bit different. He had a drawn, somewhat gaunt look, sporting quite a length of face stubble, and was hunched over his mug of warm brew. Although we were indoors and it was warm enough for me to have taken my winter coat off, he was still wearing his shabby very worn

CHAPTER 1 - THE LIFE STORY OF MICHAEL PROUDFOOT

grey raincoat. The man seemed to be a sort of down and out character, whose presence had probably been tolerated by the kindness of Joe, to sit there when the cafe wasn't busy and looking as if he preferred to be invisible.

Joe saw me looking at the man and said to me, "That's Michael; he's a very nice fellow... go and chat to him." Encouraged by that and since by nature I am a gregarious and reasonably empathetic person with a caring disposition for those less fortunate than myself, I followed Joe's suggestion and went over to the man and asked if I could join him at his table.

He looked up at me, and with a twinkle in his eyes, and a smile that went from ear to ear that lit up the room, he affably signaled for me to take a seat. We proceeded to engage in conversation, and I asked him what he used to do in earlier days. Michael told me that he had been an artist and also that his father had been quite a successful painter. Naturally, this incited my interest and curiosity. In turn, I told Michael that I too was an artist. You can check out my art at www.moichcreations.com

Then Michael told me something which really surprised me! Unlike myself, he had been fortunate enough to have had the opportunity in his youth to meet Picasso. When he told me this, I was intrigued, and this small exchange sparked a fuse that generated a connection between us.

When the winter cold made it too unpleasant for Michael

to sit outside, I occasionally found him at Piggies; over time, a warm bonhomie grew between us. Not only did I teach locally, I also lived in the area, so it was kind of 'my patch' and it was not unusual to bump into Michael when I did venture into Clapham Junction. We developed a routine of casually chatting at the cafe or wherever I came across him in town over the years. Thus, Michael became an occasional fixture in my life and I in his. Gradually, I learnt to understand him more. As the winter passed and it became warmer, I would occasionally bump into Michael standing on nearby St Johns Road.

As he sensed someone getting quite close to him, with his gaze usually averted, looking down at the floor, he would nervously, awkwardly, jerkily move away since he had a habit of avoiding close contact and definitely didn't seem to like anyone getting too physically close to him. However, as I got near him, when he recognised me, he would relax, and we would have a little conversation. He rarely communicates with anyone, but I had become an exception.

This was a fortunate experience for me as I enjoyed this special reciprocal relationship with Michael. Michael is a very unusual character, certainly a little bit strange overall. This fascinating being, if not sheltering in inclement weather in some friendly cafe, had apparently been routinely sitting or standing in a self-imposed public retreat, somewhere in the location of Clapham

CHAPTER 1 - THE LIFE STORY OF MICHAEL PROUDFOOT

Junction, for the past five decades! Since initially meeting Michael over three of those decades ago, my job has changed. I had retired from teaching, and over the following years, I wasn't as often in the Clapham Junction area. Thus, I came across him less frequently during those decades. Nonetheless, we had made enough of a connection for Michael to think of me as a friend.

Fast forward...

In 2019, and particularly during 2020, the year of the COVID-19 pandemic, I had more time on my hands, and I found that when I met Michael on the street, I began spending much more time with him. However, due to this pandemic, proximity to someone from a different household became an issue.

In fact, the UK Government created rules about limiting socialising, and one of these rules was referred to as a 'support bubble.' This is where a household with one adult joined with another, which was defined as a 'bubble'. Households in such a 'bubble' could still visit each other, etc., and visit public places together. Since Michael didn't have any one else, and nor did I, I considered myself at this juncture as his 'bubble' person. So, it was okay to hang out with him as it became my habit over the summer.

When we met, I would sometimes bring with me a monograph art book made by me or a book on art about some mutually appreciated artists. Perhaps you could guess who they might be by visiting my art site www.moichcreations.com. Michael would enthusiastically browse through these, after which I could usually elicit some feedback about what he had seen. As an artist, I was interested in his views and opinion on different artists. Most of our conversations were brief, with much time spent in silence. However, I also enjoyed those silent spells and the unspoken understanding within our friendship. Though Michael appeared to be just an impoverished and rather strange elderly 'street person', his presence offers far more than that. One should not judge a book by its cover, it is the same for this man.

Around the late Spring of 2020, when Michael was coming up to be 87, it transpired that I was hearing from him, many more intriguing hints about his past. So I began to think it would be interesting to make a little book about him and so I began asking Michael more probing questions about his life. This resulted in learning, for example, that his father turned out to have been a flamboyant, rather successful society portrait painter who drove Michael around, as a child, in Knightsbridge, in a bright yellow, open-top Rolls Royce; and his stepmother was a very famous actress, and so on.

I discovered that Michael had met many distinguished people in his young days, including many famous

CHAPTER 1 - THE LIFE STORY OF MICHAEL PROUDFOOT

artists. This all seemed quite incongruous from the Michael I knew but nevertheless was worth exploring. One of the pleasures of writing this book was researching some of the names Michael had given me to see their context in Michael's story.

Michael seems to have had a very unusual art-centered life up until his late twenties, and so, over that summer, we shared many a great topic of conversation, particularly about painting and 'modern' art. Even more relevant, as mentioned earlier, it turned out that both Michael and I also had a mutual interest in 'spiritual' matters.

Indeed, way back, in Michael's late twenties, around the beginning of the 1960s and the time of the Beatles and the 'All you need is Love' generation, I discovered, astonishingly, that Michael apparently frequented the same Society that I have attended in recent years myself, where the 'spiritual' topic of Non-Duality is the core focus. Relating to that, I postulated that, in his late twenties, Michael may have experienced a spiritual epiphany or even a 'spiritual crisis' - or even, as it is sometimes called, a 'spiritual awakening'.

It seems that sometime around that period, or into his thirties, Michael began to adopt a lifestyle which for all intents and purposes, was that of a 'street person'. In a way, living by 'simply being' like, a sort of urban sadhu. With these insights, I began to see Michael in a different light, as being, in a somewhat strange way, a sort of

Quasi-sage. For example, Michael sometimes answered a question with a gesture of a figure pointing upwards. When I asked what his finger pointing upwards meant, Michael, replied, "Union with God".

Stepping aside from that for a moment, going back to Michael's very early life, with his parents' marriage being 'dissolved' when he was only three years old, then being looked after by his grandmother and spending most of his youth in boarding schools, sometimes having unhappy experiences there, perhaps you might recognise a classic possibility of childhood trauma. There is a certain feeling of him being damaged by his early experiences.

It is no wonder that he grew up into a very introverted young man, later even being diagnosed as apparently having symptoms of chronic schizophrenia. However, that being said, that's not all there is to Michael, for there is a silver lining to this story. Despite exhibiting, in later years, an outer careless appearance of a somewhat lost soul and living a fragile fragmented sort of life, Michael appears to have found an internal way out of all this to live continually in the present moment in a reconciled and contented way, with profound peace and happiness.

In some ways, the tale being told may not always read like a conventional linear story[1]. The process of

CHAPTER 1 - THE LIFE STORY OF MICHAEL PROUDFOOT

acquiring information whether factual or not from Michael as similarly stated elsewhere was like separating the wheat from the chaff. It is more like a kaleidoscope of tatters, a patchwork of familiar ghosts.

Footnotes:

1. There were so many short anecdotes, almost like a sort of a 'quiet Tourette's, streams of consciousness. There were so many little mirror fragments of different shapes and sizes, not exactly making a pretty necklace but more of a shaman's string of memories, evoking past ghosts as if they were living in the present, haunted experiences and reoccurring blips of memory.

CHAPTER 2

Ancestry

"Don't be dead serious about your life. It is just a play."
Sadhguru

To explore Michael's roots, we need to dip into some ancient history and look at the antecedents of the three main characters in Michael's life, namely his father, his mother and his father's second wife - Michael's stepmother, who he sometimes referred to as his aunt. So, starting with his parents, these were the Gosmans of Newcastle-Upon-Tyne and the Proudfoots of Perth, Perthshire in Scotland. Michael's father, James Proudfoot, was born on the 3rd of March 1908 in Perth, Perthshire, Scotland.

The name Proudfoot was widespread in England in medieval times, before it entered Scotland. In those days, the Kings of Britain used to take census rolls to determine how much taxation their subjects should pay. These formed the first records where the Proudfoot name could

CHAPTER 2: ANCESTRY

be found. It certainly was recorded back in the 13th Century. It seems that the surname is derived from a nickname given to a person who walked with a strutting, arrogant gait, a familiar and colloquial term for a haughty man. Apparently, Michael's father James may have turned out to deserve that nickname to a tee, though Michael told me that he was a wonderful man.

Other variations of the name are Proudfot and Protfot. Though most prevalent now in the United States, the highest density of families with the name of Proudfoot were found in Scotland.

Due to the 'dissolution' of his parents' marriage before or when Michael was about three, he was looked after by his paternal grandmother, that is James's mother Annie Bruce, but sadly, not a lot of other information about her was found. Apparently, Michael was also looked after by a friend of his father's, called Erica who had a daughter named Judy. Michael was about six and Judy was about two. Michael said, "I used to look after her." However, by the time Judy was sixteen, he never saw her again.

Regarding the early origins of Michael's mother; the Gosman family is quite interesting. Editha or Edith May Gosman, Michael's mother, was much later known as Elisabeth or Lis to Michael. She was born in Westgate, Newcastle-upon-Tyne, Northumberland around 1912.

A bit of history on the origins of the name Gosman is

worth exploring and for those interested, you can find further detailed investigation, you are invited to visit my upcoming website at www.moichcreations.com.

It was quite a surprise when Michael related a story to me (which he said was told to him by his mother) regarding her family history. She told him that the family name was originally Guzman. The surname Guzman had potentially sounded more romantic than the Gosmans of Newcastle- Upon-Tyne. Perhaps Michael got his facts confused, though he has a surprisingly good memory - or his mother had. However, the story was an intriguing one. This is a remarkable account involving Spain's highest aristocracy. According to Michael, his mother thought she was descended from Gaspar de Guzmán, known as the Count Duke of Olivares, a Spanish royal favourite of Philip IV and Spanish Prime Minister from 1621 to 1643. Velasquez painted a fabulous portrait of Count Duke Guzman on horseback. This sounds interesting but maybe the story of being a descendant is somewhat apocryphal and fanciful. Maybe just wishful thinking!

One wonders, as Michael did, about 'limpieza de sangre'. This is Spanish for purity of blood, a concept developed in 15th century Spain, referring to a person without Jewish, Muslim or un-orthodox Catholic ancestry. Purity of blood became an obsessive concern in Spain when persecuted Jews and Muslims began converting to Christianity in large numbers.

Chapter 3

Michael's Mother

"A mother can but guide - then step aside..."
From a poem by Wayne Dyer's mother[1]

Michael hasn't told me much about his mother[2], which is understandable, considering that she kind of disappeared, for a while, from Michael's life when he was two or three. Edith May Gosman, Michael's mother, was born in 1912; she may also have been known as Editha. She was born in Westgate, Newcastle-upon-Tyne, Northumberland.

Trying to fill in the missing gaps was like trying to remember details from a forgotten dream, since Michael couldn't remember much about her from those early days. He didn't say how his parents met, however, they got married in 1929. Edith was very young, only about 17 or 18. James was 21 and probably had just graduated from St Andrews. Four years later, in 1933, when she was just 21, Michael was born.

25

CHAPTER 3 - MICHAEL'S MOTHER

After graduating from St Andrews, James worked for a while in his father's carpet business designing carpets. During his spare time, he painted as much as he could. He was a very talented artist. Soon he decided to follow his dreams to go to London to further his Art studies. It is unknown what Edith was doing at that time but the marriage was 'dissolved' in 1937 when Michael was only three.

Five years later, in 1942, we discovered that Edith went on to marry a 'sailor' called Denis Norman Dyster-Clark, and he brought her to London. Michael was about nine at the time of that marriage and hadn't seen his mother for a while.

When he was about ten, around 1943, Michael attended Summer Field's School, near Oxford, and this, Michael recalled was when they reconnected; she had moved nearby and she used to come and collect him from school to spend the weekend with her.

Her marriage to Denis Norman Dyster-Clark didn't last long because soon after, she married for a third time in 1949 to Charles Henry Michael Felgate-Catt, eight years her junior. Their marriage was registered in the autumn of 1949 in Harrow, Middlesex. Her new husband worked for Cassel Dictionaries and he had a daughter Sarah E. Felgate-Catt from a previous marriage. They initially lived between South East Northwood and Ruislip. Michael recalled that his mother did a bit of acting on the stage.

In 1954 the Felgate-Cattses emigrated to New Zealand, living first in North Shore, then in Eden, in 1957, then in Waitemata in 1965; all these being in Auckland where Felgate-Catt (also known as Michael then), worked for Collins the publishers.

The time the couple spent in New Zealand was another very long gap with Michael not seeing his mum. They returned to the UK in the seventies, first living in East Knoyle in Wiltshire, in a house in the grounds of Edith's husband's parents' house. Then Edith and her husband apparently moved to Richmond and after that, perhaps to Wandsworth, where Charles Henry Michael Felgate-Catt died.

Michael used to visit them every Sunday in Richmond when in his late thirties. They had a flat at (approx) 110, Mount Ararat Road, Richmond. Edith called herself Elisabeth in those days and was known as Lis. Sadly, after a while, Michael drifted away from seeing them... his lifestyle had radically changed and he was becoming a little bit eccentric and he felt that he didn't want to worry his mum.

Michael considered Charles H.M. Felgate-Catt as his stepdad. As mentioned above, his mum and Charles probably relocated to the Wandsworth area where it is recorded that Charles died there in 1988 when Michael was approximately 58. At that time, Edith and Charles probably hadn't seen Michael for many years. Since

CHAPTER 3 - MICHAEL'S MOTHER

Michael's mother and stepfather were probably residents in or near Wandsworth, this may account for Michael's attachment to that area.

Footnotes:

1. From the book Wisdom of the Ages - 60 Days to Enlightenment by Wayne W. Dyer, publisher Quill, an imprint of HarperCollins Publishers, Introduction XV.

2. Michael's mother told him that her father, Edward Murray Gosman, made paintings of peeled oranges. Michael never met him. His mother pointed her father's paintings out to Michael when he was very, very young when they lived in Perth. It must have made a huge emotional visual impression on him at that young age. I said to Michael, "The story about your grandfather reminds me of your sketches or paintings of lemons". Apparently, Michael's only solo Art Exhibition in his late twenties was mostly sketches of lemons and oranges. "Oranges and lemons, the bells of St Clemens," Michael quoted back to me.

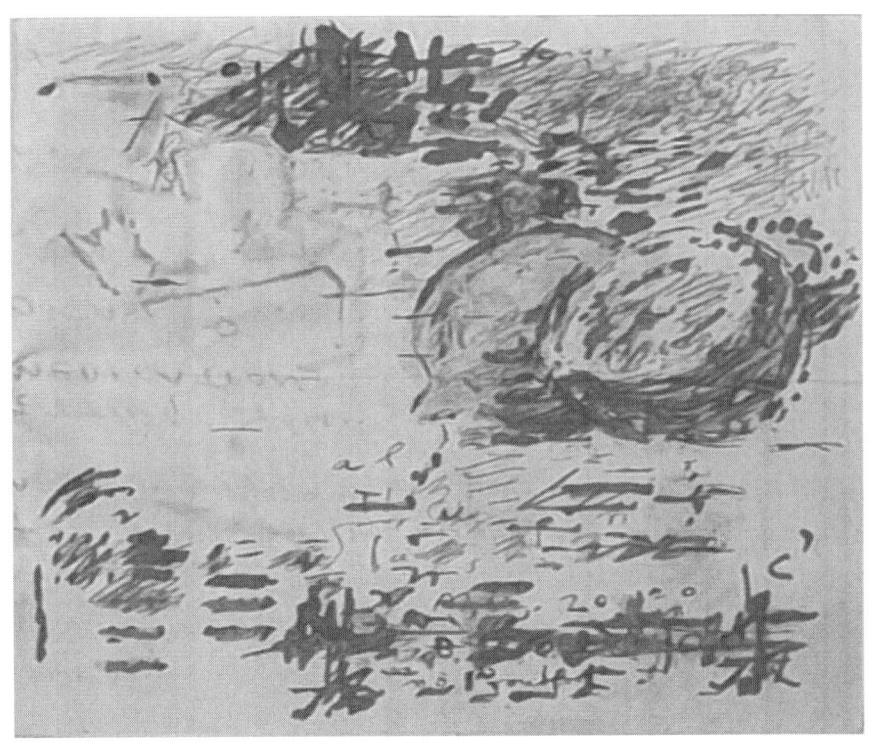

A drawing of lemons that Michael made in his eighties.

Chapter 4

Michael's Father

"Enlightenment is learning to stand on your own two feet."

Adyashanti

"A most reasonable man," Michael said, looking at a picture of his father, "though you can't tell from the photo," he added pointing at it. James Proudfoot was born in Perth, Perthshire, Scotland on 3 March 1908 and died in London on 15 July 1971.

James was educated at Perth Academy. He married Edith May Gosman in 1929. They had a son, our Michael Proudfoot, on 5 May 1933. James worked for a short while designing carpets in his father's carpet business.

From two paintings done around that time, one can see that he was very talented and they indicated that

CHAPTER 4 - MICHAEL'S FATHER

he had ambitions to become a serious artist. One painting was a self-portrait, oil on canvas (1935), and the other was Perth Rooftops, oil on canvas, painted around January 1936. It seems that probably during that year, James was off to London.

This was a turning point in Michael's life. From what I managed to gather; this is what seems to have emerged. For unknown reasons, the marriage to Edith May Gosman was dissolved in 1936 when Michael was just three.

This must have been a confusing time for Michael because by the time he was four, he was being looked after by his grandmother in Perth and at that time his parents were no longer around.

James's ambitions to become a successful artist had led him to apply to Heatherley's School of Fine Art in London where he studied during the autumn of 1936. By 1937 James had permanently settled in London and was studying at Goldsmiths College, approximately from 1937 to 1940. Incidentally, from 1980 - 82, I did my MA in Fine Art there, 4 years before Damian Hirst.

In 1937 James painted a well-received portrait of the celebrated stage actress Ellen Pollock. This connection eventually led these two to become a couple although, at the time of the portrait, Ellen was married to Colonel Leslie Frank Hancock with whom she had a son also called Michael.

Early in 1943, James painted a portrait of his son, our Michael, aged nine. James was by now becoming a celebrated artist sporting a red beard and for a while, he drove a yellow Rolls-Royce convertible, which Michael remembers being driven around in, in Knightsbridge, London, when he was about ten.

James Proudfoot served during the war, in the army, as a camouflage expert. Quite a contrast from his yellow Rolls- Royce.

Ellen Pollock's husband tragically died in Normandy in 1944 and James married her in 1945.

He was a dashing figure and became a well-known society portrait painter and a member of the Royal Society of Portrait Painters. He also liked to play the banjo and smoked a Meerschaum pipe. Michael said that he shouldn't have been smoking as he had asthma. Michael's father did indeed smoke a Meerschaum pipe but was Michael confused about him smoking a similar one in Paris in spite of his own asthma?

James had many stars of stage and screen amongst his patrons and he exhibited at many prestigious exhibitions including the Royal Academy, the Paris Salon, the NewEnglish Art Club, and the Royal Scottish Academy, receiving an honorable mention for his portrait of Peter Ustinov at the 1956 Paris Salon.

James had a renowned sense of humour and executed many comic drawings and caricatures which he termed

CHAPTER 4 - MICHAEL'S FATHER

Proudfootery. Many of his works can be found in the Perth Museum and Art Gallery. James died on the 15th of July 1971 when Michael was 38.

Throughout those last years, Michael rarely saw his father saying that he didn't want to disturb him. Certainly, Michael's life was becoming very different from the way his father knew him when he was younger.

To see loads more awesome material which I couldn't fit into this book, copy the following link: www.moichcreations.com into your web , for example, a very helpful Family Tree diagram about key relationships in Michael's life.

Chapter 5

Michael's Stepmother

"I know of only one duty, and that is to love."
George Bernard Shaw

Michael's father remarried in 1945 to Ellen Pollock, a beautiful and very talented woman, who was born in Heidelberg, Germany in 1902. Michael said she was German-Jewish. Thus, she became Michael's stepmother – Auntie Ellen, as she was sometimes known to Michael.

Ellen Pollock's mother, Hedwig Kahn, was the sister of Otto Hermann Kahn (a wealthy investment banker, collector, philanthropist, and patron of the arts) and composer Robert Kahn.

Though, of course, not a blood relative, here is a little speculation about Ellen Pollock's surname. Since Ellen was born in Heidelberg, Germany, the name Pollock could well have been derived from 'Pollack'

CHAPTER 5 - MICHAEL'S STEPMOTHER

However, since Ellen arrived as a little girl in London sometime between 1902 and 1907, one wonders how her mother Hedwig Kahn met her father! And was he a Pollock from Germany or from the UK, perhaps even Scottish? This too remains a mystery.

James and Ellen remained married until James Proudfoot died in 1971. She met Michael's father around 1937 and he painted a beautiful portrait of her. Ellen was married at that time to Colonel Leslie Frank Hancock from 1929 until 1944 when he was killed in Normandy. They had a son Michael Hancock circa 1929/30, born three years before our Michael Bruce Proudfoot.

Michael Hancock had quite a role in Michael's life, for example, when Michael's father got together with his stepmother, Michael was sent to the same school as the older boy, Ellen's son.

Whilst being interviewed on Desert Island Discs, BBC Radio 4, Ellen once recounted that she had decided to be an actress when she was only five years old. She said this was after seeing Sarah Bernhardt on stage at the Coliseum in London. Ellen had her first theatrical appearance, aged 17, at the Everyman, Hampstead and a few weeks later shared the stage with Ellen Terry.

Starting at the age of 18, Ellen joined a company touring all over the UK and abroad, exclusively performing plays by Bernard Shaw. From this, she developed a lifelong passion for anything to do with Shaw. In fact, in a long career spanning seven decades, she played more Bernard Shaw heroines than anyone else.

She also directed the London seasons of his plays and had the honour, from 1949, of being the President of the Bernard Shaw Society. From early in her career, Ellen appeared in many West End productions, some of which she directed. She was a highly versatile and distinguished character actor in just about every genre you can think of.

Ellen was also an important drama teacher where she taught at the Royal Academy of Dramatic Arts and at the Webber Douglas School of Acting. Late in her stage career, she appeared in television plays and series, including The Forsyth Saga. She had also appeared in films starting in 1927 with the silent movie Moulin Rouge, and later Piccadilly (1929), The Informer (1935), The Galloping Major (1951), and Too Many Crooks (1958). Ellen appeared as the celebrity guest for Desert Island Discs in 1970.

Twenty years later, in 1992, she appeared in the British TV series 'This Is Your Life' presented by Michael Aspel who turned up at her stall in Antiquarius Antiques Centre in the King's Road, clutching that famous Big Red Book. Ellen had set up the stall with her sister Nancy. Appearing in 'This Is Your Life' was a wonderful treat for her 90th birthday. She was thrilled

CHAPTER 5 - MICHAEL'S STEPMOTHER

to be able to enjoy watching excerpts from the popular movies in which she performed when she was younger and in the surprise company of many of her old friends. On one occasion, Michael recalled, his stepmother acted in a play at the Grand Guignol Theatre in Paris; Michael further told me that he went with his stepbrother to the play.

Ellen died on 29 March 1997.

Back to Michael's story...

Chapter 6

Schools

"The only education is enlightenment."

Lailah Gifty Akita

Pre school

In my opinion, Michael had a rough deal when he was little. His parents were about 21 and 25 when he was born, and sad to say, they were soon to separate and, in effect, to disappear from Michaels life like a mirage. What caused the breakup of the family is uncertain, but by the time Michael was three, the marriage had been 'dissolved.' Annie Bruce, James's mother, became Michael's carer and James left home to go to London to pursue his interest in art.

After a while, James brought his mum and Michael down to London too. He arranged for them to live in a house,

CHAPTER 6: SCHOOLS

which he bought, in an outer suburb of London called Sunbury. However, James had other plans for himself; while Annie Bruce and Michael were to live in number six, Manor Drive, Sunbury, James was living in Chelsea, in the middle of London, in the centre of the art world.

Michael told me, incidentally, that at some point, he was also being looked after by his father's 'friend' Erica. The absence of parents, especially his mother, must have greatly affected the little chap.

Year	Key Events
1929	Parent's marriage - Edith May Gosman (17), James Proudfoot (21)
1933	Michael born 5 May - Edith (21), James (25)
1936	James goes to London - marriage 'dissolves', Michael (3), James paints Ellen Pollock 1937
1936-1943	Michael (3-10) looked after by dad's friend Erica and grandmother Annie Bruce Proudfoot
1942	Having moved to Sunbury on Thames, Edith remarried to Denis Norman Dyster-Clark, London
1939-1943	St Teresa's Primary School (Nuns), Sunbury on Thames, Michael (6-10)
1943-1946	Summer Field's Boys Boarding School, Oxford, Michael (10-13)
1944	Ellen's first husband dies, Normandy
1945	Father marries Ellen
1947-1951	Cheltenham Boys Boarding School, Michael (14-18)
1949	Edith's third marriage to Charles Felgate-Catt, London
1953-1955	Michael goes to Paris and Spain and meets Picasso, Michael (20-22)

Primary School St Teresa's

Michael said that at about the age of six, he went to a local co-ed school, the nearby St Teresa's Primary Catholic School in Sunbury, London, which was run by Catholic nuns. This was Michael's first school. He was there from the age of six to ten.

Schools run by nuns at that time didn't have great press as the discipline imposed by them sometimes became abusive. In that respect, in terms of the trauma experienced in Michael's childhood, it may be worth noting that Michael also boarded there when his grandmother was not well.

However, St Teresa's doesn't seem to exist now. A St Ignatius Catholic Primary School near Manor Drive in Sunbury has probably replaced it.

It is interesting how some memories stay vivid. It's the little things that matter. Michael recalled that there was a girl named Brenda when they were about six, who sat at the desk behind him.

Moving on, after St Teresa's, Michael was 'dispatched', for most of his teenage years, until the age of 18, to boy's boarding schools. An account of his memories from those days follows below.

A boarding school is a school where children live in the school, away from home and their families, for quite long stretches of time. As such, a boarding school

CHAPTER 6: SCHOOLS

education is known to be more challenging than a private day school or ordinary local school. Incidentally, in Michael's case, his boarding schools were actually rather special, even quite famous.

These boarding schools are sometimes referred to in England as Public Schools, an antiquated term because, paradoxically, they are not for the ordinary public but for the children of parents who could afford an expensive private education for their children. Nowadays, they mostly prefer to be known as independent schools.

Michael's father, James, must have been doing well financially with his portrait painting commissions, despite it being wartime. Perhaps he also inherited money from his father, Michael's grandfather, because James was now able to give Michael what is considered a first-rate private education. Also, Michael told me, that after acquiring the house in Sunbury, his father bought several more properties.

It seemed that Michael was a shy lad. And from what he hinted at, some of his experiences at these famous single-sex, boys boarding schools were undoubtedly challenging for him and sometimes disturbing. Consequently, I think young Michael must have withdrawn into himself and became more introverted.

Summer Fields

After St Teresa's, at the age of ten, Michael was sent to the first of these expensive boarding schools called Summer Fields. It was an independent boys' boarding school in Oxford.

Summer Fields was known as a 'Prep' or preparatory school, a type of school where upper and upper-middle- class families sent their children to prepare them for their secondary education. As mentioned, this was curiously known as the 'public' school system, actually being 'private' and fee-paying, as distinguished from local government free state schools.

He remained there from 1943 to 1947, during and just after the end of the war years, until he was thirteen. This is also the time that Michael's father married for the second time, in 1945. Hence, it was a very influential period in Michael's life.

Summer Fields was founded in 1864 and had as its school motto: 'Mens Sana In Corpore Sano - A healthy mind in a healthy body', reflecting the diverse interests of the Summer Fields founders, Archibald and Gertrude Maclaren. The motto had made such an impression on Michael that decades later, he would still use it as a response at times when asked, 'how are you?': " Mens Sana In Corpore Sano" he would say.

When Summer Fields started its long history,

Archibald was a fencing master who founded and ran

CHAPTER 6: SCHOOLS

the Oxford Gymnasium and believed very much in the efficacy of sport; his wife Gertrude was much more the academic, thoroughly versed in the Classics and a gifted teacher.

Before the war, it was a bad time for Prep schools with low admissions. When the war started in 1939, three other private schools were evacuated from their location to combine, integrate and merge with Summer Fields, allowing it to thrive.

For the young Michael, arriving at Summer Fields in 1943 aged ten must have been a very different experience from his primary school in Sunbury on the Thames with the Catholic nuns.

He had his first piano lessons at Summer Fields, which led to a lifelong enthusiasm for tinkering on the keyboard. He studied music there with a music teacher called Duerincz.

Another subject that Michael found interesting was Latin. He sometimes came up with a Latin word or phrase. Michael loves to use quotes in foreign tongues, whether they be Latin, Greek, French, German, or Italian.

Demonstrating his Latin vocabulary, Michael referred to himself as a 'senex,' meaning an old man. When I commented "I don't see an old man. I see an eternally youthful spirit," Michael's reply was, "Let's hope so," followed by an expression which Michael often comes up with, "Chi Lo Sa?" which is Italian, meaning 'Who knows?'

'Neco' was another word he sometimes came up with. 'Neco' means 'Kill' in Latin. Michael sometimes referred to concerns about topics related to that word, especially in relation to its opposite. Michael was adamant about not harming or killing any 'microorganisms' as he would call the tiny creatures that he would spot crawling around on the floor when he was sitting outside somewhere. He had a remarkable aptitude for spotting them. This also applied to mice that infested his previous flat in Connor Court. No comment.

On one occasion, asking Michael to let me out of his new (mice-free) flat, he came up with 'Servus Nobis januam aperuit'... 'Slave open the door for us', following this with an explanatory comment about January being the door of the year. These strange connections that Michael so often came up came up with were a little like clues to a cryptic mystical crossword puzzle. Another latin phrase 'I've heard him use was 'Agimus tibi gratias' - meaning 'we thank you,' said in grace before and after a meal, not that I noticed Michael saying grace.

Here's another strange one, when much older, Michael needed the antibiotic ciprofloxacin because he had an infection. Making these weird connections between words, he remarked 'bulpes' was another name for ofloxacin (though I couldn't find any verification of that) and then rhymed 'Vulpes', which means 'fox' in

CHAPTER 6: SCHOOLS

Latin, and something about hiding the fox. I didn't exactly follow that one. However, perhaps it was Michael being psychic, because, curiously, I sometimes paint pictures with foxes in them and I was born in a place called 'Fox Holes.'

Nancy Mitfords, who became a renowned novelist, Michael recounted, was also at Summer Fields. Other fellow students at Summer Fields included Michael Player, of the famous Player cigarette dynasty and Desmond Guinness, whose family made their fortune in beer. This was when Michael was about 10 or 11. Telling about that, Michael went off tangentially and mentioned a 3000-year-old Egyptian picture of a girl making beer that he had seen. Michael said that he played tennis with Michael Player however, Michael said he himself preferred table tennis. Regarding sport, Michael said it was a terrible mistake changing the game of football to rugby football because he preferred football.

Sopwith was another pupil at Summer Fields; his family built airplanes in the 'first world war'. Harold Macmillan was there too. He became Prime Minister. Other boys with families with brand names included Lucas (electrical manufacturers), who had a chic record player. "Chic is a French word meaning elegantly and stylishly fashionable," Michael said, "and is pronounced as 'sheek' and not 'chick', so you can sound as chic as you look."

Some more names Michael mentioned were Ferguson

(also electrical), and Jimmy 'Jam' Hartley. Michael thinks that David Sylvester, who became an art critic, may also have been there. Quite a few of these went on to Eton. Michael went to Cheltenham. A boy called Charlie Gilby was there - his family had something to do with gin manufacturing.

Intriguingly, Michael's father chose Summer Fields because his future wife, Ellen, had already sent her son there. Evidentially, the canny James, thought it wise to send Michael to Summer Fields as well, to keep in with her. To prevent confusion, since his future step brother had the same name, our Michael was called Bruce.

After his father had married Ellen, both boys being in the same school made sense, and this continued into his next school.

His stepbrother used to play the song 'Trout' by Shubert on the piano, Michael recalled.

Cheltenham

When Michael was about fourteen, he continued his secondary education at the Cheltenham Boys Boarding School, another distinguished private or 'public' school. This was from 1947 to 1951, until Michael was eighteen years old. The school was founded by G. S. Harcourt and J.S. Iredell, two Cheltenham residents, who founded it in July 1841 to educate the sons of

CHAPTER 6: SCHOOLS

gentlemen. The school later became known simply as Cheltenham College. It was originally divided into Classical and Military sides until the mid-twentieth century. Cheltenham is one of only three schools in England (the others being Eton College and the Duke of York's Royal Military School) to have its own military colours. I wonder how much of a military ethos it still had in Michael's time there.

When Michael was sixteen, he broke his nose whilst at Cheltenham. He said it was an accident and that it bled profusely. He remarked that the same thing happened to Michelangelo. Michael told me he enjoyed playing football especially when playing against the Dragon School. There were also many famous students and alumni who attended Cheltenham.

Michael's quoted a few boys with well-known surnames. Michael told me that Tim Henman, the famous tennis player, who though as a young chap was diagnosed with a type of bone disease had carried on playing tennis anyway and became a professional aged 18 in 1992, and a champion. He was there no doubt a lot later than Michael. During Michaels time, there was Timothy Nott-Bower, the son of the then Chief of Police. Incidentally Michael said Timothy means 'Fear of God'. There was a boy who Michael played cricket with, who had the surname Dick. Michael wondered if a recent Chief of Police, Commissioner of the Metropolitan Police Service in London, Dame Cressida Rose Dick DBE QPM was his daughter! There was a chap called Prince Sapiea. He was a friend in later times of Mrs Nell Dunn, who was also a close friend of Michael, as discussed elsewhere. Michael reminisced that he saw various ex-students, including some from Summer Fields, at Nell's place and that Nell's father had "something to do with steel".

Obviously, there were many more boys that he knew there but for some reason his recollection of school mates from his time in Summer Field was more vivid... Perhaps some things took place amongst the older boys, Michael one time hinted about, at Cheltenham which he preferred to forget or even block out from his memory? In every case, Michael said that the teachers were very 'reasonable'. "I liked all the teachers; I couldn't find any blame for any of them."

Dr Müller was his German teacher; a wonderful, very reasonable person, said Michael, and very easy going. He taught Michael from the text: Deutsche Abend; this led to Michael enjoying quoting German, like 'Eigentlich' meaning 'actually' and for some reason the German word for hyphen fascinated him - bindes frich. "I am very fond of German," said Michael.

Other subjects that interested him were French and English. "My English teacher was Mr Moseley," said Michael. "His daughter; who attended Cheltenham Ladies College, which was nearby, came in one day to speak to her father. She was wearing a green

CHAPTER 6: SCHOOLS

uniform with a middle length skirt," he added. She evidently made a good impression on Michael as he described her as 'quite attractive'. His maths teacher had the nickname Rumble Toes. Michael loved art, of course, and the art teacher might have been a Mr Bell. One of the sports teachers was Mr Brown, who ran in the Olympics. Michael also enjoyed running, especially the 220 and 440 metre races. "Were you any good?" I asked, "Not unreasonable, of course", said Michael.

Michael's favourite pastime at Cheltenham was table tennis. "You have to practise a lot. No practice, no win." Michael also liked swimming and later, on a trip to the South of France, he swam there too. However, Michael said, "I wouldn't do it now because I'm never quite sure where the sharks are!"

Now some good news to share. Michael told me that although, after the 'dissolution' of the marriage, his mother may have been no longer there for him, nevertheless his parents remained friends, yes, I hope that was true, and Michael regained the connection with his mother again later.

When Michael was about 10, his mother eventually went to live and work in Richmond, she would fetch him from school to spend weekends with her, He could remember her speaking to the Headmaster Mr Evans, a very reasonable man, Michael said. His mother had a gramophone record player and used to play songs for him; like songs by the famous singers Jean Sablon and

Frank Sinatra. Clearly, it was during those visits to his mother, that Michael got his interest, and may I say, his passion for music.

However, whilst going away to boarding school later, when he was a bit older, he was distracted, and for a while, forgot about this interest, until he realised, as he said, he 'needed' it as a hobby.

His father remarried, to the glamorous actress Ellen Pollock, when Michael was 12, and his stepmother became known to him as his 'Auntie'.

Skipping ahead, after leaving school, when Michael was about 20 to 22, he went to Paris to study art. Though mainly staying in that wonderful city...he occasionally travelled elsewhere in France and even met Picasso!

During those travels, Michael also spent a short time in Spain.

Later in life, Michael began drifting away from family connections and even from living a conventional life style in the sense of having a proper home and roof over his head. Some of the responsibility for this was no doubt due to Michael's somewhat fixated attitude of 'I don't want to be a bother, or to cause any trouble', and therefore self- inflicted. *"The one thing one doesn't want to share is one's poverty,"* Michael said to me.

Chapter 7
Life in Chelsea

"An era of creativity where intellect and art converged."

Anonymous

After Cheltenham, the teenage Michael was mostly with his father in Chelsea, London.

When he was about 18, Michael attended the foundation course in Chelsea Polytechnic which later became known independently as the Chelsea College of Arts. Dame Elizabeth Frink, the famous sculptor and printmaker, was there between 1949 and 1953. She might have been the fellow student who reputedly drew on the walls.

Another teacher from Chelsea, Robert Medley, artist and theatre designer, made a memorable impression on Michael. Medley was a friend of Pulitzer Prize winning poet W.H. Auden and had been the first person to encourage Auden to become a poet, when they were at Gresham's School together. Medley taught at Chelsea until 1949 and was also a visiting lecturer at the Slade,

CHAPTER 7: LIFE IN CHELSEA

where in 1958, he became a full-time Head of the Department of Theatre Design - a post he held until 1966. He often visited Chelsea during the time Michael was there and they were friends.

Michael told me that when he was having tea with Robert, Medley had talked about his friend Sir Jacob Epstein KBE and his son Theo. Sir Jacob was an American-British sculptor who helped pioneer modern sculpture.

Michael commented that Robert also had letters after his name.

On occasion Robert invited Michael home. He had his drawings on the wall which were quite sophisticated, said Michael. One day internationally famous Henry Moore turned up. This was when he was managing the placing of one of his sculptures, relocating it outside the Arts School, in Manresa Road. There's another one in a London Park which is totally different to the one outside the Polytechnic, which is now Chelsea School of Art.

Around that time, the college employed teachers like Henry Moore and painter Graham Sutherland. Also, Ceri Richards, an imaginative Welsh painter who became quite famous, having worked in the Tate Gallery, taught there too.

Michael once commented about his father to me. "My father was a really wonderful man, you can tell that from his paintings," Michael said. His father's studio was

Fabulously located in a building called Trafalgar Studios, which also accommodated the studios of several other acclaimed Chelsea artists. Positioned just off the King's Road, on Manresa Road, it was in the epicenter of creativity, standing boldly opposite the Chelsea College of Arts. Once, Robert Medley visited the studio to look at his father's work. Whilst there, he noticed sketches that Michael had made and commented perhaps somewhat over succinctly, "Commercialise!"

Trafalgar Studios were a set of purpose-built artists' studios where a number of notable artists worked. The three-storey, 15-unit block was built in 1878 by John Brass. They were the first such studios in London, but further blocks were built nearby, attempting to emulate their success. Chelsea was the artistic centre of London, and there were hundreds of studios, many around Manresa Road. Chelsea and the Kings Road area have been buzzing with vitality since Michael's time there in the fifties. Michael told me that he still thought of Chelsea as his artistic 'home'.

Michael once mentioned an illuminating connection with a girl called Bunty. "No, she was not Billy Bunter. She was in fact an attractive lady, nothing to do with Billy Bunter. She looked after me, providing me with meals, sometimes baked beans, in a place somewhere near my father's studio," said Michael.

Another time, Michael was telling me about the war. At

CHAPTER 7: LIFE IN CHELSEA

one time they could clearly hear the whining sound of a German V bomb rocket as it flew to its target, buzzing above them.

Michael said "No, no, no. Don't write that down." Which he sometimes said when seeing me scribble a particular note whilst he was talking... Nonetheless, I said that this was interesting. He went on to explain that Anna, an ex-girlfriend of mine whom he had met back in the 80s, might be offended since she was German. I told him that at that time Anna was actually embarrassed about being German and in denial of it. In fact, she hid her nationality from me saying that she was Dutch. She happened to live in the Netherlands at that time.

The point of Michael saying, "no, no, no, don't write that down," was another example of his extreme sensitivity to not wanting to hurt the feelings of anybody which went along with his concern not to kill micro-organisms. This characteristic reminded me of the Nobel Prize winner Dr Schweitzer who when living in the African jungle didn't want to kill any small creature, even a mosquito as it was life and therefore had to be respected. According to him, the purpose of human life is to serve, to show compassion and the will to help others.

Another story Michael threw into the pot was about Hildegard Knef, a famous actress, who once turned up at his father's studio. Probably to arrange to have her portrait painted. She was an alluring blonde leading actress in a number of Nazi propaganda films whose performances in two post-war movies caught the eye of producer David Selznick. Knef's refusal to change her name or conceal her past stymied her Hollywood career, though she appeared in several European productions in the fifties and through to the seventies.

Michael said his father had a reproduction of John Tunnard in his studio. Tunnard's earlier style featured landscapes, marine scenes and still lifes. Later in the 1930s, his style changed to surrealist abstraction, when Tunnard began to paint works influenced by the styles of Joan Miró and Paul Klee, embracing the so-called School of British Surrealism.

I don't know what prompted it but one day, Michael told what appeared initially to be a joke. I guess this story or joke may have been triggered by us chatting about his father's house which must have had three floors. The Trafalgar Studios in Manresa Road apparently also had three floors. Michael recounted the story like this: "My father's house was imaginary and in darkness. An imaginary black bloke went up to the first floor, somebody called out, "Who dat?" He ended up on the second floor. Another voice called, "Who dat?" He went up to the top floor. The bloke responded, "Who dat who said who dat?"

Sounds strange and not in good taste, I thought. Later, I

CHAPTER 7: LIFE IN CHELSEA

was browsing through Michael's favourite book, by Ouspensky, called 'The Fourth Way'. That book was probably Michaels 'Bible' around the time he was 29 to his early 30s. I concluded that Michael was in fact

alluding to a metaphor described there, about 3 stages of spiritual development, illustrated by ascending three floors, in the darkness.

He's often mentioned the name of that book to me and now I could see how profoundly important that book was to his big shift in Consciousness.

Analysing further the story Michael told I could indeed see it was like a parable of the stages of spiritual development as referred to by Ouspensky, but put in Michael's highly veiled way, essentially presenting a teaching that only one without prejudice could appreciate. The last line of his 'joke': "He went up to the top floor. The bloke responded "Who dat who said who dat?" is perhaps about enquiring into the later stages of our so called enlightenement, asking the question, "Who is there?" and saying that unless one enters the light of realization that nobody is there, one is still in the dark dream of delusion. Still the matter of poor taste in choice of words is arguable.

Trafalgar Studios was the studio of many well-known Chelsea artists, including that of Michael's father. Similar to the numerous anecdotes highlighted in this book, the ones being shared here are drawn from peculiar fragments or odd snippets gleaned during conversations with Michael. These instances often emerged, for example, while discussing art books I might have shared with him, appearing as seemingly random recollections or Michael enjoying wordplay. He often talked about events which happened more than 60 years ago as if they were in the

present. Typically, Michael would sometimes, as mentioned, by interjecting odd remarks, create very bizarre connections between his interests and memories, and what we were talking about. Michael often appeared to be talking to himself. To bring him out, I sometimes butted in, to attempt to create more of a two way conversation. I did this, by repeating back to Michael a word or phrase I heard him say to himself. "What did that mean?" I occasionally asked.

And then Michael would include me in and explain some little details which led to interesting anecdotes. hA neat example of this could be seen here. Michael said, "My father spent his life in taverns. I occasionally accompanied him to the Queens Elm in Chelsea. Tavernier Taverns... get it?" Michael was referring to the French merchant Jean-Baptiste Tavernier (1605–89), who in his book 'Travels to India' wrote about his interviews with many seventeenth century Indian mystics and sadhus. He wrote about their yoga practises holding one or two hands up vertically - a version, they told him, of union with Brahma. This was a favourite topic of Michael's and a yoga practice

CHAPTER 7: LIFE IN CHELSEA

which he himself embraced for the rest of his life.

Regarding the Queens Elm, Michael said that a certain Colonel Daryl Brown was often there often too, because it was right next door to where he lived. What interested Michael was that the Colonel had a daughter who was the same age as himself, and he thought that she was very attractive. Her name was Penelope. Incidentally, the pub is now converted to a clothes shop. An ignominious end; to the once renowned Queens Elm - the former haunt of writers and artists and one of the half dozen London Courage pubs that retained its hand pumps during the keg revolution of the early seventies.

Here's another example from our strange little exchanges. We were looking at a book of Modern Art and came across a Giorgio De Chirico. Michael said, my father's name Proudfoot relates to Chiropody and is therefore related to De Chirico's painting 'Chiropedic'. A bizarre, surrealistic observation. I asked "Did your father tell you that or did you work that out for yourself?". "I worked it out for myself," replied Michael. "Have you got nothing better to do?" I commented. We both laughed.

Like Michael, De Chirico was fascinated with language[1]. De Chirico was also a writer, Michael said. At least, Michael added, De Chirico wrote one surrealist novel called Hebdomeros.

Another key location and favourite place to hang out for his father James, which was located very near his studio and occupying the same house in Old Church Street since 1902, was The Arts Club in Chelsea. Its members from all fields of the arts include film makers, writers, actors and musicians. Michael was occasionally taken there by his father, even from a young age, or met him there when he was older, and was introduced to many interesting people some of whom were already very well known - and not only artists. Michael recounted how at the age of ten, on one visit there, he shook hands with Professor Alexander Fleming, who discovered penicillin, for which Fleming was awarded the Nobel prize. Fleming would have been about 62 when Michael met him.

Michael was with his father in the garden at the Chelsea Arts Club, when John Rothensten, Director of the Tate at that time, came along and spoke to his father. I wonder what about? Michael told me he used to see the painter John Craxton around Chelsea and also had met him in the Arts Club. He must have liked Michael because he gave him a drawing. When Craxton was younger, he had attended the Académie de la Grande Chaumière in Paris, which Michael attended later. He had also attended Goldsmiths which was something he had in common with Michael's father. Michael said that once John Craxton was jokingly pretending to be Eduardo Paolozzi - a curious titbit between friends.

I think Michael also loved poetry and told me about his near encounter with T.S. Eliot during Eliot's time in

CHAPTER 7: LIFE IN CHELSEA

Chelsea. From 1946 to 1957 Eliot lived quite near his father, in Carlyle Mansions, Chelsea and then in Kensington. Michael said that he saw him going into a church in Southwell Gardens. Eliot had parked opposite Michael's dad's home. Michael mentioned that when T.S. Elliot died in 1965, his ashes were sent back to St Louis, his birthplace.

Because of his love of music, Michael must have also been delighted to have met and spoken to David Jacobs who was involved with the Light Programmes Pick of the Pops and the Eurovision Song Contest.

Another friend of Michael's father was the actress Hermione Baddeley. One of her most important roles was in Brighton Rock (1947), in which she played Ida, one of the main characters. Through his father, Michael also met actor Robert Newton who starred in the film Treasure Island, and also Dennis Price (Kind Hearts and Coronets and No Orchids for Miss Blandish).

The great art teacher and painter, Ceri Richards was also mentioned - possibly because of his connection with Chelsea Art College, as was John Minton, another famous painter who held the rank of guardsman in the army. Michael had observed that Minton seemed to be in need of money and was at the time with the singer Annie Ross. Michael mentioned that he also shook hands with Dylan Thomas, (Do not go gentle into that good night ...) when he was with his father in the Six Bells pub in Kings Road, near Oakley Street.

Sir Kenneth Clarke's daughter Collette Clarke, turned up with a friend of Nell Dunn, who famously wrote 'Up the Junction'. More about her later. Michael's father used to say to him, "Your wish is my command." I asked Michael what he meant. "Ah! that famous phrase from a certain daddy?" His answer to what he was asking him for was, "Almost certainly lemonade".

Talking of lemonade, the film star Trevor Howard's girlfriend Helen Cherry, a famous actress, once bought Michael a lemonade from a pub near the Queen's Elm in Chelsea.

Perhaps this was when Michael was younger and on a visit to his father. Helen used to live with Ellen Pollack or had something to do with her! Michael sometimes went with his stepmother to The Ivy Theatre Restaurant, in Covent Garden, one of the grand dames of the London restaurant scene, a long-standing celebrity haunt in art deco surrounds.

Michael's dad was financially quite acute. He had sharesin whiskey and owned a few properties. Talking about whiskey, Michael mentioned that one day while Michael and his father were on the bus, they bumped into Jack Daniels known as the whiskey king. Hearing this, I was prompted to ask Michael, "Was there anyone else, more contemporary, that you would like to meet?" Michael replied, "I am happy if I can breathe".

CHAPTER 7: LIFE IN CHELSEA

As mentioned before, Michael often came up with odd facts that sometimes, I was uncertain whether they were true. Such an example was when Michael said "Ben Nicholson's wife had triplets." Michael also told me that the artist David who was Ben Nicholson's cousin had met with Michael and also that David had met with Rita, his father's model. Michael was one of Rita's male friends and sometimes he danced with her. She often helped Michael with somewhere to sleep, he told me. It seemed that Michael collected these apparently random bits of information, like a magpie collecting shiny trinkets. Michael exclaimed again: Alle Seiten. Excitement! Everything goes!

Quite often there was a discussion as to whether to have coffee or tea. Michael once intoned: "I love coffee, I love tea. I love Java Jive; Java Jive loves me." Michael recounted that Rosalind, the mother of Matthew Collings, an art critic and artist, taught or explained to him about yoga or the benefits of raising the arms for some periods oftime. She explained to Michael what the physical effects of the yogic position of holding the hands up vertically are. "Hande Hoche!" meaning 'Hands up', Michael liked to exclaim in German.

Michael saw a picture in the metro paper of a young ballerina with hands up in the air in a Sauté and he kept telling me that he thought it was very funny. Of course, that's in reference to him holding his hand or hands up, either doing his 17th century yoga practice or the Tadasana joga pose, a sort of yoga Palm Tree. These are different from his hand gesture with index finger pointing upwards symbolising 'Union with God'.

"These arm positions are very, very funny," said Michael while showing me the photo in the newspaper again.

Michael said, "We can only become conscious beings if we use energy in the right way which is at present being used in the wrong way," and he followed this up again with his familiar Hande Hoch! This idiosyncrasy of Michael's reminds me of Marquis Joe Scicluna of Malta, who was another friend of mine before he passed away. He was a great eccentric who loved to dress in khaki army uniform throughout his life. I took him out for a drive one day and he would give directions 'Army left, army right', as we drove along.

Michael's father was also a friend of Sculptor Jacob Epstein, who Michael met, with his father, in Kensington Gardens Park which is a great place to meet people. Theo Garman, Epstein's son, was there too; he was also a painter and incidentally had taken his mother's name. Also, Epstein had his daughter Esther with him, who tragically committed suicide.

His other daughter Kitty was married to Lucien Freud, who could also be seen often in the Chelsea Arts Club. Lucien Freud painted a picture of Kitty with a white dog. Michael was about twenty at the time and this was

CHAPTER 7: LIFE IN CHELSEA

shortly before he went to Paris with his father.

A curious thing Michael recounted was about a Terracotta figurine of a 2000-year-old goddess, which Michael eventually misplaced. This was given to Michael by the fascinating Mrs Kathleen Garmen, who became Epsteins third wife. Kathleen began a relationship with the married sculptor Jacob Epstein, in 1921, becoming his model and his mistress. One of the many intriguing tales about her was that in 1923, Epstein's jealous wife Margaret invited Kathleen to her house and shot her in the shoulder with a pearl-handled pistol!

Regarding the loss of the figurine, Michael said, I am an Ass. Michael then came out with a very long quote from, 'A Midsummer Night's Dream', no doubt identifying with Bottom.

Footnotes:

1. As mentioned, a favourite phrase Michael used was Chi Lo Sa? (Who knows?) He often used this enigmatic Italian phrase to express the unknowability of even something mundane that we were discussing. I had mentioned to Michael that I was interested in learning Italian, but had told him that I had procrastinated. There was a course available which entailed just three minutes a day. He would sometimes nudge me about this by asking for example, "How many words in Italian do you know?"

Chapter 8

Paris

"If you are lucky enough to have lived in Paris as a young man, then wherever you go for the rest of your life, it stays with you, for Paris is a moveable feast."
Ernest Hemingway, A Moveable Feast

On many occasions, when we chatted in Clapham Junction, Michael would come out with anecdotes from the time when he was about twenty, when he accompanied his father on an exciting trip to Paris and afterwards stayed there on his own for a couple of years. What follows are some snippets gleaned from those conversations.

The Paris trip was in the 1950s which turned out to be one of the happiest periods of Michael's life. I listened with great interest as he recounted very vividly places that he had been to, or people that he had met there, more than six decades earlier. Here are some of the people that Michael mentioned.

CHAPTER 8: PARIS

Michael's father had apparently arranged for Michael to lodge in an apartment in Montparnasse with a lady called Ida Karsky or Karskaya, whereas the father, only staying for a short while whilst Michael settled in, took residence in a smart five-star local hotel called the Hotel Georg V in Avenue George V, which still is in business today. "My father and I were dining at La Coupole, 102, Boulevarde De Montparnasse," Michael said. With its art deco decor, historical heritage, it is the legendary Parisian brasserie frequented by a who's who of Parisian artists and characters such as Edith Piaf, Ernest Hemingway and Serge Gainsbourg. While they were there, Jean-Paul Sartre passed through. La Coupole translates as 'The Dome' in English, but it is not to be confused with the nearby Dome restaurant at number 108, which was another famous Montparnasse restaurant.

Edith Piaf was a French singer-songwriter, cabaret performer and film actress noted as France's national chanteuse and one of the country's most popular international stars. Her most widely known songs include La Vie en Rose and Non, je ne regrette rien. Ernest Hemingway was an American writer who won the Pulitzer Prize (1953) and the Nobel Prize in Literature (1954) for his novel The Old Man and the Sea, which was made into a 1958 film with the same title.

Serge Gainsbourg was a French singer-songwriter, pianist with many other talents. He was regarded as the most important figure in French pop whilst alive, sadly ending up as an alcoholic. Jean-Paul Sartre was a philosopher and leading existentialist who dealt in his work with the nature of human life and the structures of consciousness. He refused the Nobel Prize in Literature in 1964. Interestingly, one of his notable works, a treatise from 1943 was called Being and Nothingness.

Another time, whilst having coffee, the amazing Juliette Gréco was sitting diagonally opposite them in St Germain. Michael confessed with some remorse, "I didn't speak to her". Gréco was a devotee of the bohemian fashion of some intellectuals of post-war France. She was a friend of Jean-Paul Sartre, who commented Gréco had "millions of poems in her voice". She was known to many of the writers and artists working in Saint-Germain-des-Prés, such as Albert Camus and Jacques Prévert gaining the nickname laMuse de l'existentialisme.

Gréco was often to be seen frequenting the Saint-Germain- des-Prés cafes, immersing herself in political and philosophical bohemian culture. As a regular at music and poetry venues like Le Tabou on Rue Dauphine, she was acquainted with Jean Cocteau and was given a role in one of Cocteau's films, Orphée (1950). She had a famous affair with US jazz musician Miles Davis but they decided to stay just lovers because their careers were in different countries and his fear of damaging her career by being in an interracial relationship. They remained lovers and friends until his

CHAPTER 8 - PARIS

death in 1991. "My dad also had a jeep", Michael told me. "I remember him standing in the jeep in Paris, in the Avenue des Champs-Élysées, Paris, painting." Michael's father returned to London and over the following two years Michael stayed on in Paris. He continued to be supported by his father, although returning to England for a short visit occasionally. During his time in Paris, he took a trip to the French Riviera, staying in Cannes and also went to Spain for a few months.

After his father left, Michael continued his stay in Montparnasse with Ida Karsky or Karskaya. She had a son a bit younger than Michael. A woman called Monique was a friend there too. Ida Karskaya is first and foremost a "character" as one Parisian art critic wrote in the first biography to be devoted to the artist. The critic went on to describe her as: "A sort of dandy who could sport a romantic cape and lace jabot with as great an ease as the unique outfits she designed for herself."

Born in Bessarabia in 1905, the young Ida Schreibman went to Belgium in 1922 where she studied medicine. She moved to Paris in 1924 and specialised in psychiatry. There, she associated with the Russian bohemians. In 1930 she married the painter and journalist Serge Karsky. She began to paint in the 1930s and exhibited at the Salon des Tuileries in 1936. She was encouraged by her friend, Chaim Soutine, to pursue her artistic endeavours.

Michael attended a sculpture class at Academie de la Grande Chaumière, Montparnasse. He learnt to work with clay and to make armatures for his sculptures. Teachers there around that time included Ossip Zadkine, who was perhaps just before Michael's time, and Jean Metzinger.

The Academie was a centre of social and artistic life for many artists, writers and philosophers in the area. It was a favoured place for Modigliani, Miro, Lempicka and Louise Bourgeois. Former British students included Alexander Calder, Isabel Rawsthorne, as well as John Craxton, another acquaintance of Michael from London.

Michael used to go to nearby Wadja's Café, which still exists, at 10 rue de la Grande Chaumière. Wadja is a bistro type restaurant that is tucked away in a little side street in the Montparnasse area on a historical site located next door to the Académie de la Grande Chaumière and is where starving artists once used to go for a meal. This authentic and small bistro still has an almost 1930s look with the original tiled floor and lots of pictures decorating the walls.

There, a sequence of serendipitous meetings became life-changing events for Michael.

He met Francois Jeze, a sculptor, who became a very special friend. Michael often mentioned his name to me but I could not find any record of his work. I think he was a fellow sculpture student at Académie de la Grande Chaumière. Michael talked about Jeze a lot, in a rambling sort of way, like this: "Jeze and his wife, Paulo, were about to have a child, though I never got to see the

CHAPTER 8 - PARIS

child. Jeze used to do ballet as well as make sculptures. To get to the place where Jeze did his sculpting, we used to go right through a bakery to get to his studio".

Michael told me also: "Jeze's father worked in the Renault motor car industry and his grandfather had two sisters, with whom he was living".

Jeze later came to London and met Michael's special friend-girl, Nell Dunne. 'Friend--girl' was Michaels term for ladies he felt connected to[1].

Francois introduced Michael to Solange Lubtchansky. She was married to the filmmaker Jean-Claude Lubtchansky. She was a very important influence in Michael's life. Michael got the first 'moves' of what he referred to as the "the game" from Solange. "On Joue, (French, meaning, it's only a game) it's no good taking things too seriously," he said. Solange showed Michael the yoga practise of holding hands and arms stretched forward. "It's only a game," Michael would often say. Nevertheless, this and similar yogic exercises mentioned earlier, derived from 17th century yogis, would become a life-long practise of Michael.

I asked Michael, "Which spiritual teacher alive or dead has made the most impression on you?" "Jean-Claude Lubtchansky, Solange's husband", Michael said. Lubtchansky had instructed Michael, "get things tighter, (then) it's a different world". This evidently made a huge impression on Michael. No doubt, these words of wisdom, were related to Lubtchansky's experience in film. He co- edited the famous film 'Lord of the Flies'; Solange was also credited as working in the editorial department of that film. He was also in the production team of 'Meetings with Remarkable Men'. His film 'The Seekers of Truth', has been reviewed as arguably the best film ever about Gurdjieff.

Michael loves music and went to hear the clarinettist Sidney Bechet, when Bechet moved from America to Paris. He was one of the first important jazz soloists whose recordings precede those of Louis Armstrong (three years his junior) with whom he would later play duets.

In 1953, in Paris, Bechet had a recording contract with Disque Vogue. They recorded many hit tunes, including Les Oignons, Promenade aux Champs-Elysées, and the international hit Petite Fleur. He also composed a classical ballet score in the late Romantic style of Tchaikovsky called La Nuit est une Sorcière (The Night is a Witch). Some existentialists in France took to calling him le dieu ("the god").

Monique or Monika was German woman, another 'friend- girl', who made Michael cabbage soup. She brought Michael a dictionary as well as magazines and cigarettes from Germany. Hence, perhaps Michael's use of the German word for cigarettes. Michael said, "You would have loved Monika, a lovely person. She

CHAPTER 8 - PARIS

was also the girl who let me in Madame Karsky's (or Karskaya's) house in Paris when I arrived there."

According to Michael; Madame Karskaya, who became his friend in Paris, was a charming woman who had made wonderful abstract paintings in her studio in Montparnasse. He also spoke of another friend Madame Guertich, who he visited regularly for tea at an apartment nearby in Rue Georges Sand. She translated Henry Miller and they talked about Charlie Chaplin, who she described because of his slapstick ways as a cabatin, a ham actor.

Michael also mentioned George Sand and her romantic connection to Chopin.

An art exhibition going on at that time in Paris that interested Michael featured 'Crows' by the artist Bernard Buffet. He went to see both second and third exhibitions in Paris by that artist. He particularly admired Buffet's rendering of the crows. "I've never seen better", said Michael.

One of Michael's great pleasures, later in life, was feeding crows. He seemed to develop a special relationship with them, and loved sharing his lunch with them. Michael had commented to me, whilst feeding crows, "the food isn't regular enough for them, it's not breakfast, lunch and dinner."

Michael smoked in Paris; he smoked a pipe similar to his father's Meerschaum. Demonstrating his interest in languages, Michael said the German for cigarettes was cigaretta. And that was the important word for the day. C'est Du Noire Gauloise - Gitane. (It's Gallic Black – Gypsy). "Picasso liked those," Michael remarked. Yes, in fact, Michael smoked[2] into his late twenties and despite having chronic asthma, he said he didn't regret it.

How different Michael's thoughts were in his later life regarding being near people who smoke. In the time I have known Michael, whenever somebody started smoking in his vicinity, he immediately had to move away... because of his asthma, he said... pointing and muttering "smoker, smoker". This regularly happened in one of his favourite haunts, where he fed the pigeons and crows. This place was often invaded by smokers. Michael has a special inhaler spray for his asthma and would then need to use it. While discussing inhalers Michael enigmatically said, "Rain doesn't agree with inhalers. Water and air might be devastating".

In Paris, Michael thought he met his friend artist Tony Kingsmill. Back in England, Tony had later introduced Michael to another well-known painter Keith Vaughan.

Also later, Michael told me, his friend in Paris, Solange, came to London. There, she told Michael that if he wanted a free meal, he could go to Luba Bistro in Knightsbridge, near Harrods. One of the nieces of Gurdjieff had some connection there. Perhaps she owned it. Did Solange tell you about Colet House? I asked Michael. "Possibly," said Michael.

Visiting Spain

Whilst living in France, Michael took a few short trips to Spain. A couple of French girls from the Arts School in Paris, probably from the sculpture class, took him there on a short holiday. One was called Laurence. Michael didn't tell me the name of the other friend. They took Michael with them to Madrid and went to a bull fight. "That's a bit cruel," I said. "Tell that to the crowd at the bull fight," replied Michael.

Michael also went to Spain on a different occasion with his friend Jeze and again to Madrid and the Prado. He also visited Castel de Fels on the coast near Barcelona near Sitges. Michael rented a villa from a friend of a friend of Jeze who then came to stay with his wife. She was probably pregnant at that time because Michael referred several times to her daughter which he never met. Michael didn't tell me much about his visits to Spain. I got the impression that what interested him most were the beach and the sea.

Meeting Picasso

Towards the end of his stay in France, Michael made a trip south to the French Riviera, to Nice and Cannes. He wanted to see the sea and to swim. Michael also visited the

Picasso Museum in Antibes and liked the drawings of Centaurs. When he was in Cannes, he also knew or heard that Picasso was living there, in a place called Villa La Californie.³ He looked in a phone book and Picasso's phone and address were listed there. So, he decided to ring him up.

A strange conversation ensued. The person on the other end of the telephone asked what he wanted and Michael said that he wished to visit Picasso. The person on the other end of the line told him that Picasso was not there. "Lui n'est pas là." "Tant pis" replied Michael "Too bad."

He asked Michael to tell him from where he was. Then the person said, "I am Picasso!" and then Picasso said to Michael to come to such an address at such a time on the following Sunday afternoon. The conversation, of course, was in French. When Michael arrived there, a gate opened and Michael joined a queue of visitors waiting to have an 'audience' with the Master, possibly around 15 to 20 people. Picasso had a special pencil which could write automatically in different colours.

After each conversation Picasso would autograph for them a postcard or similar item, of his well-known bunch of flowers. When it was eventually Michael's turn, Picasso took Michael's hand in his and the first thing Picasso said to Michael, in French, was "Do you know Douglas Cooper?" Cooper was a British art historian, art critic and art collector and a friend of Picasso. He then gave Michael one of the cards, autographed it for him.

CHAPTER 8 - PARIS

Picasso was a serious advocate of peace, Michael added. Jeze really liked Picasso's work. When Michael told him, that he had been to see Picasso, Jeze couldn't believe it. Michael had originally gone to the South of France for the sun, the beach and the sea near Cannes but found a much brighter 'star', Monsieur Picasso!

Footnotes:

1. friend-girl... see next chapter

2. When he was with his stepbrother, they smoked a brand called "Passing Clouds". Michael said he smoked "Just a few cigarettes". Because he had asthma, he realised eventually that he ought to smoke less, because "Life is precious".

3 Villa La Californie, also known as Villa Fénelon, Villa Picasso, and now known as Pavillon de Flore, is a villa in Cannes, France. The house overlooks the bay of Cannes from Le Suquet. In the background are the hills of the quarter of Californie, which gave its name to the villa. It is located at 22 Costebelle Avenue. The villa was built in 1920 and was the main residence of artist Pablo Picasso from 1955 to 1961. Pablo Picasso had already been installed in La Californie since the 1940s, but in 1955 he bought the house and moved there with Jacqueline Roque. It is from this workshop that he painted the Bay of Cannes, in 1958, where he represents the seascape strangled by the urban environment. In 1961, when the construction of a new building concealing the sea view, Picasso decided to look for another home.

He left the house in Cannes and moved to Mougins, where he spent his last years. During the inventory of Picasso's estate, many previously unknown works were found in the house and formed part of the original collection of the national museum which bears his name. His granddaughter, Marina Picasso, inherited Californie and finished restoration work in 1987. She renamed the villa as Pavillon de Flore. (Wikipedia)

Chapter 9

London in the 50's

"In London, love and scandal are considered the best sweeteners of tea."

John Osbourne

Memorable encounters

Michael recounted that a date marker for that period when he returned to London after his adventures in France may have been when he was around 23. That would have been circa 1956. He recollected to me the story of one of his homes in London at that time. Understandably, Michael's memory of events more than six decades earlier was sometimes quite hazy. Nonetheless, he clearly remembered the name Brian Desmond Hurst. Reminiscing on this, Michael mused, "Was I in his apartment - or was it the other way around?" Belfast-born Hurst, who later became a famous film director, had over thirty films in his filmography. He was a most prolific Irish film director during the 20th century and hailed as Northern

CHAPTER 9: LONDON IN THE 50'S

Ireland's best. Michael mentioned a film he made called Dangerous Moonlight (1941).

Apparently, the actor Sir Michael Redgrave was a mutual friend. While tinkering at a piano, probably in the apartment or a nearby pub, Michael said that he 'nearly' sang Mel Torme's song 'You stepped out of a dream', to him. The actor must have impressed Michael.

Music was always important to Michael. Patrick Bashford, a friend, who played Spanish classical guitar, and was a professor at the Royal College of Music, took him along there to a concert one day.

Sleeping here and there... Locations where Michael lived:

Michael slept in his dad's studio for a while, in the building called Trafalgar Studio, on Manresa Road. As mentioned previously, one day Henry Moore popped in. They were setting up a work by him outside Chelsea Art school, on the other side of the street. Michael was about 24.

For the following decade Michael had a nomadic sort of life, living in many different places. He lived in Herne Hill in a house owned by Michael Piarle, an Irish bus driver from Birmingham who owned the house but lived in Chelsea. Michael Piarle owned quite a number of houses. He was a very shrewd man, said Michael.

Another time, when Michael didn't have anywhere to sleep, the father of his friend Nina, who may have had the surname Hobbs, and was an artist to some extent, had put Michael up for a night or two in his place in Battersea. Nina was blonde. She reminded Michael of the Vermeer painting of a girl with a pearl earring. Michael also used to visit singer Annie Ross's flat in his twenties.

Michael recalled that he once lived somewhere near Kinnerton Street in Belgravia.

Michael also told me that used to visit his friend Baudie Duerinx, a Belgian man who played classical guitar. He kindly gave Michael the key to his flat when Michael needed a place to stay. There was also a lady there, with a 10-month-old child, Michael said.

Another memorable time, his Summer Fields school chum McGuiness gave Michael a place to sleep on his houseboat on the River Thames near Lots Road. This was an important period because Michael painted whilst on the houseboat for an upcoming solo exhibition.

More substantially, Michael rented a room from Mrs Mary McKierne at 59 Candahar Road. She didn't live there. Michael lived there for maybe eight years. After that, he lived with Mrs McKierne in Sisters Avenue, maybe for one year, until her daughter returned with the children. She helped Michael to find a place in Arun

Lodge, Earlsfield, near Earlsfield Road. After that, Michael moved to 26 Connor Court on Battersea Park Road.

One time, Michael made a very revealing comment "I'm not really interested in males... one of my kinks... it makes me rather nervous." This probably harks back to his school days in Cheltenham, where he had been abused by a classmate, which clearly had a lifelong affect on him. However, he was always happy when referring to his 'Friend – Girls'.

Friend-girls rather than girl-friends

Michael's 'friend-girl' Nina, as he called her, was about his age. She was blond, and Michael recalled he was too uneasy to look at her closely. So we see Michael was quite shy! He also insisted that she was only a friend and that his fondness for his top favourite song, 'Nina never knew,' is only a coincidence. When I asked about this, discountingly, Michael said "The song is American, I am English, and Nina is English. It doesn't remind me of her, even vaguely," he said. "Check the lyrics for yourself." Do we believe him?[1]

A German woman Monika, another 'friend-girl', was also often mentioned.

Michael had an 'affair' with a girl called Barbara, who also painted. He lived with her for a few days. They held hands sometimes but never kissed. After telling me this, he insisted they were only friends.

Michael had been to the Ritz in Piccadilly a couple of times with the surrealist painter Leonor Fini, who is considered one of the most important women artists of the mid-twentieth century. He may have met her in the 1960s when she exhibited at the Kaplan gallery in 1960 and the Hanover Gallery in 1967. She was an Argentinian surrealist painter and also a designer, illustrator and author who was known for her depictions of powerful and erotic women. She was once photographed nude in a swimming pool by Cartier-Bresson. The photograph of Fini sold in 2007 for $305,000 - the highest price paid at auction for a photo atthat time.

A friend of Michael's stepmother Mrs Adulesco owned a Matisse, and on another occasion, she was with Michael's stepbrother having lunch again in the Ritz. "She was probably wealthy, otherwise, she wouldn't want to be in the Ritz. You can't be in the Ritz without money. Money is the root of all blessings", Michael said. Ironically? I responded, "I have to check that name." Michael retorted, "Go to Czechoslovakia!" "check-slovakia... get it?" said Michael.

Michael also knew Rita Wheatley, his father's model.

Rose Reckitt was the daughter of the man who manufactured vitamin E45s. Michael met Rose Reckitt through Nell, at a wedding reception at the Ritz. This was the wedding of Nell to Jeremy Sandford, who

CHAPTER 9: LONDON IN THE 50'S

wrote Cathy Come Home, a 1966 BBC television play directed by Ken Loach about homelessness and arguably one of the best British television programmes ever made. Jeremy was married to Nell Dunn from 1957 to 1979.

Up the Junction... Nell Dunn

Nell Mary Dunn was roughly the same age as Michael. She was born in 1936 and was about three years older than him. She was a very successful screenwriter, playwright and author. Amongst others, she wrote Up the Junction and Poor Cow, directed by Ken Loach, and Steaming. Incidentally, she was the maternal granddaughter of the 5th Earl of Rosslyn - the man who broke the bank at Monte Carlo! Nell's father, Sir Philip Dunn, did not believe that his daughters needed any qualifications, and, as a result, Nell had never passed an exam in her life.

According to Nell, her father wanted them all to be unique. Although she came from an upper-class background, Dunn moved to Battersea in 1959, where she worked for a time in a sweet factory. Michael had met Nell Dunn via his painter friend Donald Camille and Michael and Nell became good friends.

Life in Battersea inspired much of what Nell Dunn would later write. Michael was about 27 at the time.

It transpired that Michael stayed with some 'mysterious'

friends in Wiltshire; that is, he refused to mention who they were. Nell Dunne's mother was there for a while, but Michael didn't want me to mention her by name either. They were Aristocrats! Apparently, Michael was offered some film work whilst he was there with Nell.

Another time Michael clearly mentioned going to Wiltshire with painters Robin Campbell (Arts Council) and Duncan Grant (Bloomsbury Group), whose names he didn't censor. Michael knew Robin Campbell through Nell. The film director Brian Desmond Hurst could have been at the Ritz wedding too. He was mentioned earlier. In Nell Dunn's house, Michael met John Bratby and Peter Blake, both famous painters. Nell Dunn's sister Serena was married to a Rothschild. They may have lived in Deodar Road in Putney, where Nell had moved to.

Later, back in London, there was also a girl called Yara who was the Brazilian wife of a German man and who worked in a cafe called Westies in Wandsworth. Michael used to go there all the time. "It was quite far to go... some distance," he said.

I'm not sure if Michael said that he knew Vera Lynn, the singer and 'Forces Sweetheart', famous for entertaining the troops during the Second World War. Perhaps it was another Vera. At one point, he did mention her. This was quickly dismissed. Michael said that we are not allowed to write down a lot about the

CHAPTER 9: LONDON IN THE 50'S

'friend-girls' as "that causes trouble". We were talking of events which occurred about sixty or more years ago!

Solo Exhibition

When Michael was about 27, he had a solo exhibition. Michael painted for his exhibition whilst staying on a grand barge in Cheyne Walk near Lots Road in the late fifties or early sixties.

It took Michael about six months to finish his painting project. The barge belonged to his old schoolmate, McGuiness, who he had met again in a cafe in Chelsea. His staying there might have had something to do with Jeremy Sandford and Nell Dunn. Had it cost him anything to stay there? "Neco nil," Michael said.

Michael used to go for coffee to a place near the river Thames, Cheyne Walk, he recounted. He was hanging around outside what appeared to be a furniture shop, but it turned out to be a taverna. Michael was invited in by the owner, a gentleman by the name of Mr Smart. At that time, Michael lived on Stadium Street, near Lots Road. An American lady, Mrs Rothschild, was also a customer. Michael knew Serena Rothschild, her daughter. She was also a regular there. Prior to her marriage into the Rothschild Dynasty, her surname was Dunn. She was the sister of Nell Dunn, who wrote 'Up the Junction'. Mrs Rothschild used to ask Michael, "How are you?" and he'd reply, "Could be worse". She replied, "You always say that!".

Little is known about Michael's first and only solo exhibition. However, he told me that a friend called Prince Ibqual or Iqbal came to the exhibition.

Apparently, all of Michael's works were sold! The gallery art dealer Dick Temple, Michael insisted, was not crooked, yet Michael contradicted himself by saying that the dealer stole all the money from the exhibition. He then confused the matter even more by saying that the dealer used the money to pay for Michael's accommodation after the show.

Chatting about property and jobs

Once, Michael was looking at the Evening Standard Property Section at a page of adverts by estate agents Dextor's, "I suppose looking at one page may be as good as looking at another", he quipped. Incidentally, I knew that Michael had very little money as I had often helped him get his pension from a cash machine as he didn't know or want to know how to use a bank card.

Back to the ad. Michael pointed out a figure of a property price showing there, with lots of noughts, asking me, "is that a million?" which I confirmed was the case. I told him that he wouldn't like it there, it wouldn't suit him, and it's not the familiar sort of place which he was used to. He commented, "Not bohemian enough."

CHAPTER 9: LONDON IN THE 50'S

"Did you ever have a proper job?" I asked Michael.

"On and off," was his reply. Michael, said he helped a Greek grocer on Falcon Road in exchange for groceries.

There may also have been an Indian grocery shop on Falcon Road that Michael used to help to clear up at the end of their day.

Michael also told me that he 'worked' in the Cuba Bistro Restaurant, which was owned by Luba, or Lubja, one of the nieces of Gurdjieff. Michael occasionally did the parsley preparation in her restaurant. That was his little job. Luba's restaurant was very near to a bridge, possibly Battersea Bridge.

Another little job Michael had for a while was 'selling potatoes' in a Greek grocery shop on Falcon Road for one or two days a week. He got the job because he was a good customer, However, this job didn't last long. Michael said, "because there were other applicants with CVs who were more into nutrition than him."

Somehow, there was a connection there via Solange, who, at that time, was into Fitness First and Pain Therapy.

More memorable encounters

Michael told me that around 1964, Paul McCartney had invited him along to the Apple office in Saville Row, where he met Mick Jagger. David Litvinoff, another acquaintance of Michael, was there also and asked Michael, "Do you want a word with Paul McCartney on the telephone?" Mick Jagger came in with John Lennon and Yoko Ono. Michael was holding his hand up in a yoga position when he told me this anecdote related to when he was around 31. Litvinov was described by his niece Vida as "the court jester to the rich, smart Chelsea set of the 60s". Apparently, he knew the notorious gangster Kray twins and was particularly friendly with Ronnie Kray. In a Times Literary Supplement from March 2016, David Collard had apparently labelled him "an opportunistic hustler". He was very well connected with famous names, but it seems he wasn't a very nice fellow.

It seems that David Litvinov was also a friend of Jazz singer and authority on Surrealist Art, George Melly.

Michael told me how he had heard George singing "Shake your Can". Michael thought it was great. He liked it very much. Melly's band had recorded a disc or CD called 'The Dark Town Strutters Ball' (Kidory). At that time George was married to Vicky... and lived in the same house in Cheyne Walk, where Michael also lived. The house belonged to sculptor and painter Timothy Whidborne who was a contemporary of George Melly at Stowe School. Timothy had been a pupil of Annigoni and, in 1969, had painted Queen Elizabeth ll on horseback as Colonel-in-Chief of the Irish Guards, of which he had once been a member. He let Michael stay in his house without charging him

CHAPTER 9: LONDON IN THE 50'S

anything. Then there was Mrs Frampton's Cosy Café. Francis Bacon, one of our most famous painters, came in, and because he was quite near, Michael heard him say on being asked what he wanted, "Tea or something", he said.. Bacon was renowned for liking alcohol. Perhaps that is why he said, "or something".

During the subsequent decade, Michael underwent a profound life transformation due to his changed outlook on life. In the upcoming chapter, we delve into Michael's newfound mindset. This shift likely originated when he encountered the writings of Ouspensky and began attending The Study Society at Colet House. It's noteworthy that this change also affected his relationships. For instance, starting around the age of 35, Michael established an 'arrangement' with his father to limit their visits, although occasional visits still took place.

Footnote:

1. See pages 168-169.

Chapter 10

Colet House[1]

"It is only when we realise that life is taking us nowhere, that it begins to have meaning."

P.D. Ouspensky

Colet House was and still is an important centre in London where, amongst other things, teachings connected with Ouspensky, were taught.

Actually, Michael never met Ouspensky, he told me.

This chapter is a bit of a jigsaw puzzle... it doesn't flow in a linear fashion but rather hops about. When you have read the whole chapter, hopefully it will have pulled itself together in your mind!

I asked Michael, "Did you remember anybody when you visited the Study Society, Colet House, Barons Court?" "There was a man called David Rawasley there. He worked for Arthur Rank film organisation," said Michael. "Then there was a Mr Tilley, who

CHAPTER 10: COLET HOUSE

possibly had a connection with a Barons Court Residence Company which may have had some connection with Colet House. Another is Kenneth Walker, who apparently was a teacher in Colet House. He taught 'Non-Duality Shine', which was mostly derived from studying P.D. Ouspensky's book called Fourth Way." I jokingly asked, "Would you like me to give you a book about the Fifth Way." Michael's answer was pretty clear. "Let me know when you have written it!"

In the conversation that followed, Michael wove together, in his metaphorical way, several topics, some quite difficult to follow. He excitedly talked about the TV series called 'The Saint' and also referred to meetings happening at Colet House, which he lightly called 'tea-parties'. These meetings were focused on spiritual development.

Anyway, I'll record it here as I heard it.

Michael mentioned that he had the privilege of meeting with Brian Desmond Hunt, the director on the TV set for the making of The Saint. Adding, "Being seen with The Saint is like getting to know the author Leslie Charteris himself".

Cryptically, he continued, "Whether it is a fictional atmosphere like in The Saint TV series or a 'tea party' at Colet House, the expression of negative emotions, or not, determines Life or Death". He seems to be referring firstly to the murder of the criminal's victims (as in The Saint), and secondly, metaphorically, to the death or 'end of our ego-centred world view'.

The 'tea-chings', hence tea-parties, at Colet House are intended to wake us up from 'separation' from 'All That Is'. Hence, a sense of 'separation' dies as it were. This often via a process called Self-remembering.

Michael continued, "Self-remembering and humility in Death and Death in humility. Concentration on death - a very cool concentration. There are different types of concentration. Deep concentration is different from surface concentration. Cool is very deep."

"If you can stop the expression of negative emotions, you will save energy and never feel the lack of it." This was an expression he often says.

Then, bringing in the crime metaphor again, Michael continued, "Every crime is merely the expression of negative emotions." Was he implying that an ego-centred world view is a crime?

"Those negative emotions arising at the Ouspensky tea parties are mild stuff, not heavy-duty crimes. These have nothing to do with a crime, such as what we see in movies." Michael jested about Dennis Walker, a habitué at Colet House, saying, "he was clearly not a master criminal. In other words, drop the gun," which he

CHAPTER 10: COLET HOUSE

explained meant to stop the expression of negative emotions, which he likened to using a sort of weapon "If you can stop the expression of negative emotions in the 'mouth of The Saint'," he continued, "it is as if asking them to temporarily discard their guns." He then added, even more obscurely, "In that situation, no blood will be poured out of the stomach. In other words, it won't be leaking holes from the gunshot wounds." These references to pouring blood, holes and leaking wounds may perhaps have something to do with Michael's health and also referencing the action between Simon Templar and Hoppy Uniatz in the Saint series.

Michael has read about ten of Leslie Charteris' books, including The Saint. He said, "I only just managed to avoid stealing from the library getting that book out!"

Michael concluded that complicated little chat by teaching me how to say 'Thank you' in Chinese... Xie Xie.

Earls Court to Barons Court

Michael lived for a while in the Earls Court area, moving to Barons Court, just around the corner from the Study Society, in Colet House. This led to a few visits there in his early twenties. What he discovered led him to buy the book 'Ouspensky's Fourth Way' written by Ouspensky, from a bookshop in Tooting. A lot of Michael's inspiration came from studying that book; it was all about Ouspensky's lectures. This began a lifelong interest in the topics discussed in that book which were ostensibly about Non-Duality.

The Study Society[2]

The Study Society acquired the freehold in 1957. This is a society devoted to studying Non-Duality. The library at Colet houses a unique and eclectic collection of some 3,000 books, journals, and audiovisual resources.

It is a valuable resource for those interested in Non-Duality and also the Arts, Science, Religion and Humanities in general.

The Society was registered in 1951 by Dr Francis C. Roles, four years after the death of his teacher, the Russian philosopher P. D. Ouspensky, who had settled in England in 1921 and died in 1947. Pyotr Demianovich Ouspensky was known for his expositions of the early work of the Greek-Armenian teacher of esoteric doctrine George Gurdjieff.

The Society was originally set up to continue Ouspensky's work as a "School of the Fourth Way". Ouspensky's teaching asserted the unity of the individual with the entire cosmos in both structure and potential.

Dr Roles continued with Ouspensky's teaching for 13 years, but in 1960, he followed Ouspensky's instruction to search for 'the source of the system'. That's another

CHAPTER 10: COLET HOUSE

story. Michael, quoting from Ouspensky, said that 'to like something' implies 'identification'. This elicited an "aha!" from me. "Ouspensky's personality was very different from Gurdieff," said Michael. "Likewise," I said, "Moich Abrahams and Michael Bruce Proudfoot have very different personalities." "And they both paint pictures," said Michael grinning.

Two key expressions from Non-Duality Advaita that Michael often quoted, were "Stop this turning of thoughts. Stop the expression of negative emotions." (Ouspensky)

Quoting Ouspensky's treatise The Fourth Way, Michael said: "One piece of the Mind thinks something, another piece of the Mind observes the thinking," adding, as often he did, the mantra "Stop the turning of negative emotions..." I asked him: "At what age did you start to practise not having negative emotions and giving up thoughts?"

"At 22," said Michael. Michael continued, "About attaining consciousness, Ouspensky wants us to be conscious of consciousness, whilst I want to be conscious of Blue Malibu!" A Michael joke?

Referring to an experience I had that morning in my bathroom, about "holding the gaze in the mirror, while the lips are asking "Who am I?" I became aware that that was just another occurrence, another case of things spontaneously arising." I said, "Upon realising this, the face in the mirror no longer looked perplexed, and a smile came into the eyes in the mirror. Then soon after, the image had gone". I asked Michael what he thought about that, and he said, "Knocks me out!". Then he added, "Yippee!" and "Preferably". I asked him what he meant, and he retorted obscurely, "super health."

Months later, the penny dropped about that phrase "knocks me out". Michael was talking about his perspective on 'being at One with God' versus the topic of 'dropping the ego'. Apparently, 'was totally enlightened', and 'knocks me out' refer to 'knocking the ego out'. Michael focussed my attention spelling out letter by letter, k-n-o-c-k-s. Although, essentially, he said it was not about dropping the ego at all but a much larger question. What Michael meant by this is not about what is not there if the so-called ego isn't in the picture but rather what IS there, namely, the Whole Universe, 'All That There Is', versus the very limited and limiting relatively tiny little world of egocentric existence. He is talking about Union with All That Is. Indeed, that knocks me out!

I understood this better later when Michael was talking about being dead in the sense that his embodied self is non-existent when absorbed in 'Union with God'.

I'm not quite sure how this came about. We were talking about 'obedience' when Michael responded, "I'm dead myself. In principle, I am dead, and humility is key. Humility in death and death in humility... It's

CHAPTER 10: COLET HOUSE

only a game, of course. The future is a result of the present.

My future is Death, so I am mostly dead now." Then Michael quoted, "Mors, Death", showing his knowledge of Latin. I deduced eventually, that Michael's attitude about being 'dead' is indeed derived from Michael's stance of 'Union with God'. To clarify, I asked him, "Has this anything to do with the death of the ego?" For example, the well-known expression, "Today is a good day to die? (a North American Indian saying), and non-dualists talking about the ego being illusory etc. Michael retorted, "Absolutely not!". I realised that he was talking from the perspective of 'Union with God', and 'All That There Is'.

So, as I understood, since there is so much of Eternity where I am not alive, this little 'life span' that we have now, where I appear to be alive, is comparatively inconsequential. We are using I in two different senses. I, the egocentric embodied being, and I, that is the Ultimate Truth of Who I Really Am - The One and Only One beyond human comprehension. So, I think I've got it! A sort of Eureka moment... Maybe.

Michael continued, in his super mysterious metaphorical way where each utterance has a hidden meaning: "No human can survive - they have to keep to the law of humility. If they don't, they may cross the road without looking. The car drivers have got more to handle than the pedestrians. They are more likely to live each day if they realise they can die. They - meaning the pedestrians. The Moon and the Sun and the Earth can't take it to live so long.

Otherwise, no 'Concentration'. Only joking, of course."

A little mixed up, but I think he was alluding to 'concentration as 'Self-remembering', i.e. remembering 'Who I Really Am'.

Footnotes:

1. We can find this very special place in West London. It is an elegant Victorian building near the underground station Baron's Court.

2. Colet House, home to the Study Society since 1957, has had a colourful history since it was first built in 1885. It has the largest single studio in London, long enough to hold a cricket pitch, and two other substantial studios. Colet has been a workplace of many artists, notably Sir Frank Brangwyn RA (1867-1956), who described it as "a wonderful place... fit for Michelangelo himself..." Sir Edward Burne-Jones RA (1833-1898), was painting there to within hours of his death. Colet Gardens got its name from the Renaissance scholar and Dean of St Paul's, John Colet, who founded St Paul's school in 1509. In the 1930s, Colet attracted emigrés from post-revolution Russia and the ballet teacher Nicolai Legat from St Petersburg established his renowned school here,

CHAPTER 10: COLET HOUSE

attracting dancers from all over the world. P.D. Ouspensky, philosopher, author and teacher of the Fourth Way, lived here before and after the second world war. Later it became home to the Royal Ballet School, guided by Ninette de Valois and Margot Fonteyn. There is an interesting YouTube video: 'Gurdjieff: The Rascal Saint – Sadhguru Exclusive' - https://tinyurl.com/2efwt5xx

Chapter 11

Spiritual Crisis & Realisation

"The game is not about becoming somebody; it's about becoming nobody."

Ram Das[1]

Michael had been concerned about an operation offered to him to remove kidney stones. He didn't want to have the operation, which was understandable for a man, at that time, of 87.

I told him about Sri Ramana Maharshi having cancer in old age and was offered an operation to amputate an arm to save his life, and that he declined.

Michael then mentioned... a Dr Jean-Baptiste Lully (1632-1687), who was an Italian-born French composer, instrumentalist and dancer who spent most of his life working in the court of Louis XIV of France. He is considered a master of the French Baroque style. He wrote a musical with 'Monsieur de Pourceaugnac', with Moliere. Michael said that Dr Jean-Baptiste was offered an operation on his foot, also to save his life – to either

CHAPTER 11 - SPIRITUAL CRISIS & REALISATION

have the operation to amputate or die, and he didn't want it.

Assumptions

Changing the subject now, I'm going to flag up the topic of making assumptions. The fact is, we often don't realise that's what we are doing! Starting with what may seem a banal or even trivial example: In the early days of my research, I assumed that Michael had spent his primary school days with the nuns in Perth, Scotland. This turned out to be an assumption which led me to have thoughts that Michael spent his first ten years in Perth. I had created, in my mind, an image of him being on his own with his grandmother in Perth and his father having gone to London. However, as mentioned earlier, what actually happened, as I discovered later, was a different story. Michael had been brought by his father at a very young age with his grandmother to a house his father had bought in Sunbury on Thames in England. He then attended the primary school at St Teresa's, in London, with the nuns there. That may sound fairly simple but it was an assumption which I'd believed for several years.

Here's another: I remember referring to a to a quote which I used as a title of one of my early art pieces, which was 'egregiously an ass', always associating it with Bottom, the ass in Shakespeare's A Midsummer Night's Dream. By the way, Michael often quotes from A Midsummer Night's Dream. Indeed, as I said, I made a sketch with that title. It was actually of a mans head with a donkey like mask super-imposed, referencing the 'Bottom' character. My assumption about where that quote came from was apparently incorrect. It turns out to be a quote from Othello, Act 2, scene 1. Incidentally, if you'd like to see some of my art works visit www.moichcreations.com

Another example: I took a journey by car to see a friend who had invited me for a birthday lunch. The previous time I'd crossed central London in my car, to the then best of my memory, the so-called Congestion Zone operated from Monday to Friday. Since this trip fell on a Sunday, I assumed that no fee payment was necessary. So, I didn't carefully scrutinise the road signs. A mistake! To my horror, 10 days later, a Congestion Charging Penalty Notice arrived, informing me that I had broken the Law by not paying the due £15 fee for crossing the zone. On researching, I discovered that the Congestion zone had been increased to seven days a week, a while back. Therefore, I had unwittingly transgressed and was asked to pay a hefty fine. I gritted my teeth and paid up. A belated undesired birthday present. Such was the cost of that minor assumption.

The topic of making assumptions could be much more serious.

A lingering - if not persistent - assumption that has actually plagued all of humanity, is the belief that males are superior to females! Really deleterious, to

CHAPTER 11 - SPIRITUAL CRISIS & REALISATION

use a favourite word that Michael and I often shared, to the welfare of women throughout history.

What about assumptions in science and human knowledge? People assumed for millennia that the earth was flat and that it was the centre of the universe. Some people may still think so. cf The Flat Earth Society.

Great insights into knowledge have often been reached through questioning assumed axioms. Einstein questioned assumptions stated in Newton's Laws and gave the world the famous mathematical equation showing how matter, energy and light are related, $E=mc^2$. This led us to understand that everything in the universe is energy-based and ultimately to the paradigm that everything is connected.

And now, let's get to it. What are the most fundamental assumptions? Could one be the assumption that I think I know who I am? I am me, and I am this body (pinching myself). We have believed, up to now, that we are these egocentric embodied, suffering characters on the stage in the play of Life. Is this assumption true?

Clearly the essential me is not my finger nails or hair, as once disposed of I am still evidently here. One could go on asking what if I lost a leg? Again, what I identify as me, is still present. One may soon arrive at the conclusion that who or what I am is something seemingly 'inhabiting' a body, which could be likened to a space suit, with lots of interesting parts. So one may deduce that the essential who or what I am is not my space suit, that is, not my body.

Coming from an Eastern tradition, the so-called 'Enquiry' into "Who am I?", is sometimes called 'The Direct Path'. That is, 'The Direct Path' to Self-Realisation', 'Enlightenement' or 'Awakening' Whatever That means!

Getting to know yourself, at this level, this investigation, could be likened to taking an unpredictable adventure down a mysterious rabbit hole.

Why ask the question; "Who am I? "

One short answer: "It is written," that the holy grail of 'peace and happiness' awaits! Hence, what Michael alludes to as a "divine game", appears worth pursuing.

For bonus info on this subject, check out, my upcoming website www.moichcreations.com

Let's move on.

As mentioned, in his early twenties, Michael discovered Ouspensky's Fourth Way, and that led to his awakening. In my case, the beginnings took place in my fifties.

I had read Marilyn Ferguson's book called 'The Aquarian Conspiracy,' which discusses that everything is somehow connected, as if in a hologram. This interconnectedness could be viewed as making up a 'unity' of all its parts. Similarly, waves in the sea are all part of the same ocean. Consider, embracing a unity viewpoint, that is, seeing things or being involved with Life, as an indivisible whole, without reference to any subject-object relations, or opposites, or aspects of the two-ness which is the marker of conventionally perceived reality. Thus interrogating a not-two or non-dual way of being. We'll shortly be using and discussing the term non-duality some more.

One could say, being awakened, enlightened, or self-realised may be likened to being a clear mirror. In Michael's case, due to emotional scars from his past, the metaphor of a 'mended mirror' might resonate better, symbolizing his resilience and capacity to 'shine'.

In the next chapter we will look at Michael's progress towards being 'nobody', in the meanwhile let's look at related topics.

Spiritual crisis

"Spiritual crisis, also sometimes called 'spiritual emergency', is a form of identity crisis where individual experiences drastic changes to their meaning system (their unique purposes, goals, values, attitudes, beliefs, identity and focus) typically because of a spontaneous spiritual experience. A spiritual crisis may cause significant disruption in psychological, social and occupational functioning." Wikipedia - Arthur J. Deikman, a clinical professor of psychiatry, coined the term "mystical psychosis". According to him, a psychotic experience need not be considered pathological, especially if consideration is given to the values and beliefs of the individual concerned. People susceptible to mystical psychosis feel a unification with society, with the world, and with God. It is characterized by easing the subject-object distinction. Deikman considered that the all-encompassing unity opened in mysticism could be the all-encompassing unity of reality. In his book, 'The Observing Self', he lucidly relates how the mystical tradition can enable western psychology to come to terms with the essential problem of meaning, self, and human progress.

The observing self, one may say, is a key aspect of the non-duality practice of 'self-study'. It is a waking state in which we dissociate from the external world and become aware of being aware, entering the day dreaming state just enough to allow us to review different aspects of reality. Is it schizophrenic the notion "I am all that there is" or even "I am God", with reference to the non-dual assertion that there is only one, not two entities? At the same time, one comes to the paradoxical conclusion of exactly the opposite, that "I am nothing". Michael has sometimes said of himself I am nothing; I am nobody. A bit more on that later.

I commented to Michael that Jesus had used the term 'I am', seven times. Michael responded, "Self remembering".

CHAPTER 11 - SPIRITUAL CRISIS & REALISATION

One of the common phenomena reported by people who talk about having had an experience of enlightenment or awakening is that they describe it as "seeing everything as one". When they talk in this manner, are they just delusional or is there more to it than that? Freud created a model of the non-dual state, based on his developmental model of the ego. Every child starts out in a state of oceanic consciousness, a sea of sensation and emotion with no boundaries at all. They cannot tell themselves from their mother, or any other outside object. The ego is essentially a boundary marker, a delineator of the self from every other thing. The development of the ego over time can be thought of as the sharpening and clarifying of that boundary.

As we grow into adulthood and our ego becomes mature, most people lose the ability to contact the earlier oceanic feeling because they cannot drop the acute feeling of separateness created by the ego. They have lost the sense of oneness with everything and are stuck in their "two-ness", as it were. Practising meditation, doing 'inquiry' and other methods, constitute a path for returning to this original undifferentiated state of mind - at least for some time.

Michael exhibits some very strange behaviours, not least of which is when he sometimes talks about not wanting to sit or be near people, in case he is accused of being a pickpocket. If somebody comes near him, he might well very jerkily step away or raise his arm and touch them as if to push them away. This could very easily be misconstrued as a sort of invasion of their personal space rather than his! Also, he can often be seen apparently talking to himself or some invisible protagonist. Michael can obsessively focus intently on the smallest stain or tiny bit of detritus on the floor.

Despite being actually highly intelligent - fluent in French, and Latin and knowing phrases from several other languages, being very knowledgeable about art and really excellent at spelling -, he also seems to have had not much interest, or perhaps ability, in looking after himself physically, in a normal way, regarding food, clothing, general welfare and other self-management skills. Even more strange is his standing in one spot for hours, somewhat like a lamp post.

All this may well fit into the conventional schizophrenia box, and certainly, Michael's early life, unfortunately, seemed to have compounded the situation, leaving him emotionally damaged, which adds to the complexity of Michael's behaviours. However, nonetheless, probably as a result of his 'awakening' in his twenties, Michael's perspective is very centred and clear on the 'all is one' non- dual paradigm, hence his "Union with God" affirmation.

Perhaps this also, in part, accounts for his other behaviours. There are many stories and cases of people having undergone a similar awakening process who have also exhibited a total lack of interest in their physical

CHAPTER 11 - SPIRITUAL CRISIS & REALISATION

welfare during the early part of their 'enlightenment' journey. In modern times one could mention Sri Ramana Maharaj and Eckhart Tolle as well as innumerable famous saints and mystics of the past, including Siddhartha Gautama, who became known as the Buddha. Isn't there a big difference between somebody thinking, for example, that they are Julius Caesar or Elvis Presley and the affirmation 'Union with God'? One might question whether Non-Duality (sometimes called awakening) is a mental disorder such as schizophrenia! Can non-dual awakening and schizophrenia be both considered as what many might commonly report as "mystical experiences"? Even William James, the 19th-century pioneer of American psychology, admitted that he had a hard time telling the difference between a 'mystical, metaphysical' experience and schizophrenia.

For someone going through stages of awakening or specific meditation-related experiences, could it be deleterious to be diagnosed and treated as if they have schizophrenia? Compare the pros and cons of medicalising such phenomena versus getting guidance from long-term meditators and spiritual teachers.

According to Non-Duality teachings, "People who think they are sane are wrong". When Michael was thirty, the same time that the Beatles were becoming popular, he spent several months as a 'guest' of the Maudsley, a famous psychiatric hospital in London. "Why were you at the Maudsley?" I asked him. "I was interested in psychology", Michael replied. Of course, I don't think he was there as a student but rather as a patient. Michael was diagnosed with chronic schizophrenia, yet he found a way to live in inner harmony with life.

Michael paid fairly regular visits to St George's Hospital in Tooting, in South London, to treat one of his several health issues, such as serious asthma or water works issues. He has worn a catheter for many years. Michael recounted was it at the Maudsley or at St George's when they asked him "to count backwards from twenty and if I knew the Prime Minister's name and other tests like that. Was this a test to see whether I was completely crazy or just checking to see if I was completely crazy?" Michael asked.

What is Non-duality?

Non-Duality is the experience of intimacy with all things, a sense of connection to and identity with the entire universe. In this experience, the sense of being a witness or seer of things vanishes completely, and instead, you feel yourself to be whatever thing you are beholding. You don't see the mountain; you are the mountain. You don't hear a bird; you are birdsong. Or rather, and more accurately perhaps, the mountain just is, and birdsong just is.

Furthermore, the thing being experienced also vanishes, in the sense that it is no longer experienced as an object nor as separate. The mountain is not a mountain; the

CHAPTER 11 - SPIRITUAL CRISIS & REALISATION

birdsong is not a thing; both are seen as vivid but somehow empty experiences.

Thus, awareness is no longer split into an experiencer and the thing that is experienced. There is just pure experience with no divisions. Experience itself, without a subject or an object, without a seer or a seen, is the essence of Non-Duality.

In spirituality, non-dualism, also called Non-Duality, means "not two" or "one undivided without a second". Non-dualism primarily refers to a state of consciousness in which the dichotomy of I versus other is "transcended", and awareness is described as "centreless" and "without dichotomies" (Wikipedia).

I suggested to Michael that, at some point, we could discuss another connection between the Atman and the Brahman. "The Atman gets up my nose," Michael said, "it's up to you". Aha! Incidentally, Michael loves to tell me about and demonstrate his 'nose yoga[2], which involves moving the various muscles in his nose in different directions.

Let's continue to dive deeper. Are there two of me? The one that claims to be me, the "I, me, mine" character, sometimes referred to as the egocentric personality - me, meaning my-self or self (with a small 's'), as one who lives in a world of duality. This 'I' is often associated with a lifetime that cannot avoid experiences of unhappiness or 'suffering'. At one time, I created an artwork entitled

'2 Heads', one being blue and the other red[3]. The red face refers to ego, symbolizing suffering. This can be viewed by visiting www.moichcreations.com

Much more mysterious, the paradigm referred to above, that says everything is totally connected, as One - the 'All That There Is', 'Isness' itself - living in a non-dual space. Did you come to the conclusion I AM that One, my-Self (with a large 'S')? Here, one has to think very differently from conventionality - in a sense, looking inwards.

In my artwork, just mentioned, the blue face, on its side, is in a more contemplative mode.[3]

Non-Duality is full of paradoxes. A paradox is something that contains apparent opposites, and the essence of Non-Duality is the union of opposites.

Michael's practice is about 'Union with God'. What does that mean?

"Eternity has worn a human face, Contracted to a little human span. Lo, the immortal, has become a man, A self-imprisoned thing in time and space". (Harindranath Chattopadhyay)

We don't normally have a chance to reflect on Divinity up close, and it is unlikely that we would recognise it if it were in front of our nose, which it actually always is. Though in plain sight, it is invisible to most.

CHAPTER 11 - SPIRITUAL CRISIS & REALISATION

Becoming nobody

Consider this metaphor: In the sense that the 'One' or the Divine or God, is working through the vehicle of the person you think you are, and is 'doing' it all, you are essentially just the vessel for the expression of that, and as such 'empty' or 'a nothing' or 'a nobody'. Hence the Invisible Man of Battersea.

If you've managed to get this far, I must also point out that this book comes with a warning. The advice is to enter the topic of self-enquiry with some degree of caution. That is, regarding Non-Duality and 'self-study', these could be considered to be very dangerous pursuits to enter into. I am not joking! This is because, in its essence, 'self-enquiry' presents a huge challenge to who you think you are, which is essentially ego based. It may lead you to go as far as putting the ego on the back seat or even melting or dissolving it away, whatever that means.

Of course, the ego does not like its position to be questioned or challenged, and it definitely doesn't want to disappear. Whether overtly or very subtly, it likes to be in control, to run the show and will surely cause havoc if its position of power is threatened.

However, the good news is that with wise self-exploration, the ego's true nature could be revealed and its tricks seen through, and curiously, it may be discovered that the ego isn't real in the first place, so maybe it's a fuss about nothing! Just to add an observation I find interesting: In the so called real world, where the ego has dominion, and thrives; like all aspects of the dual world, the ego itself, comes as part of a duality. For example, you could say that in one way, the ego is a pain, on the other hand, it is also helping guide you to be the best you can be.

As I've said, in my upcoming new website www.moichcreations.com you can find resources which looks at Self-enquiry even more fully. You can take it or leave it. Though, if you are interested in exploring your relationship to the big picture of who you really are, you may resonate with some of the many ideas mentioned.

Non-duality

This is a fascinating subject which I've been interested in for many years since being taken to a John de Ruiter 'satsang' circa 2001, which actually gave me a bad impression. I didn't like the way he seemed to encourage some of the audience to 'worship' him, especially the women who were weeping at his feet. However, fortunately, I came across the topic of Non-Duality again through meeting other teachers. Some might be referred to as gurus. Whilst considering such gurus as teachers, I didn't take them on as more than that though some had, and have, a big influence on the way I think now. Anyway, I learnt that the process, sometimes referred to as 'Self- inquiry', could be useful

CHAPTER 11 - SPIRITUAL CRISIS & REALISATION

in developing a deeper connection with Art and Life.

I continued to learn more about Non-Duality when I discovered the Study Society (Colet House), an organization which is focused on studying Non-Duality and the topics surrounding that. The enquiry or Self-enquiry centres on the profound exploration of the question 'Who am I?' and the Study Society offers 'good company' along the way.

Some great meetings take place there, my favourites are especially the Sunday discussion groups on the topic of Non-duality. Since the Covid Pandemic, these often take place via a zoom. This may be jumping in at the deep end a bit; for example, one of the presenters of the monthly Study Society Non-Duality meetings, Norman Alderton, raised the following question to be discussed: "Why do we live in the cocoon of me,' and 'my world' when the full force of unbounded Consciousness is ever available?

It became a great pleasure when I discovered that Michael had actually visited this society many years ago, somewhere between the middle of the nineteen fifties and the beginning of the sixties. Thus, I discovered that we had that interest in common as well as art. Gently over time, I started to discover much more about what really mattered to Michael and how we are on the same page about that.

In recent years, spending more time with Michael, I

came to believe that the essence of Michael's philosophy, exemplifies or manifests, in a certain way, what this practice is about. Incidentally, the in-house magazine, available from the Study Society, is appositely called 'Being'. The bottom line is 'nobody' is there, once the illusion of the ego has been realised, so indeed, the aspiration of the title of this book, 'Being a nobody', is a perfectly fitting description of what some refer to as the realised man.

To summarise. Duality means two, notable 'pairings' being 'I, me, mine', on the one side, your ego and you, on the other. Or me and the rest of the world. Non-Duality means 'not two', or one, where everything is considered as part of the one; a connection beyond conventional experience. As long as the ego is in place, maintaining its hold over so-called reality, Non-Duality or oneness, is not possible.

To summarise: Non-Duality refers to a concept, model or paradigm about 'reality', as not being divided into the egocentric two-sided apparent appearance of how things are. Alternatively, it means 'not two' but simply One, where everything that is, is understood as being totally interconnected, as a unity. Our ego-centric mind can't embrace that as it lives in a world of duality. It's literally mind boggled!

Science has come up with many models of how things are interconnected or are related, like Einstein's contribution, mentioned earlier, and for example,

CHAPTER 11 - SPIRITUAL CRISIS & REALISATION

there are models from psychology like the ones from Freud, Jung etc., but the human mind is only scratching the surface of this paradigm. This connection where 'all is one' is mostly beyond conventional experience unless one thinks 'out of the box', which in this case requires putting the ego or the egocentric view on the back seat.

Let me offer the following metaphor. Imagine a bucket which contains 'All That There Is' containing everything that could possibly be, including itself! How many such buckets are there? With calm reasoning, hopefully, the conclusion is that there is only one. Because any other bucket would also be contained in the first bucket. Let's look at this notion of 'There is only One', a unity, using the bucket metaphor. Now, stand next to the bucket and enquire, "Who am I?" Can you come up with an answer?

What you discover may seem quite crazy.

Using reason, one must come to a conclusion that 'I am the bucket'; Wow! Wow! Wow!

I am 'All That There Is'. Quite crazy. Yes, it would be to the limited ego.

There have been many names given to 'All That There Is'. I'm going to suggest one.

'All That There Is', this Unity or One, somehow takes care of itself. Using the human family as a model, we could say, for the family, the term 'taking care of itself', at the highest level, is manifested as love. Let's upscale that to also be a prime quality of 'All That There Is'. With a capital L this time. So I prefer to substitute 'All That There Is ' with the word Love.

Of course, this is a totally different use from its conventional familiar one. So we can now arrive at some amazing statements. First, from 'I am... All That There Is' becomes

the awesome statement 'I am...Love'. Taking it one crucial and vital step further, eliminating the word 'I' altogether, there is a sentence which transforms everything. That is, the mantra 'There is only Love'. The application of this statement to everything is Life transforming.

"Since everything is none other than exactly as it is, one may well just break out in laughter." (Long Chen Pa)

If you'd like to receive coaching from me on the above, to Master your own personal Peace and Happiness, you can reach me directly via

www.moichcreations.com or m@moichabrahams.co.uk

Footnotes:

1. Incidentally, there was a documentary film called Becoming Nobody, 2019, made by Jamie Catto, about the spiritual teacher Ram Dass who was originally known as Dr Richard Alpert, the eminent

CHAPTER 11 - SPIRITUAL CRISIS & REALISATION

Harvard psychologist.

2. One of Michael's favourite yoga topics, which he was quite specific about, he calls 'nose yoga'. He was punched severely on the nose by a fellow pupil at Cheltenham when he was about 15. Michael said that boy, who was a bully, thought that he was jumping the canteen queue at school, to get to the food, or nutrients as Michael called them and his nose was broken. Michael now quips about comparisons to Michelangelo, who had a broken nose too.

Michelangelo often used to get into brawls and fights, or he may have just fallen off the scaffolding of one of his awesome tall marble sculptures.

Eventually, as a result of having his nose broken, Michael became interested in the idea of strengthening his nose muscles. He found a book in Lavender Hill Public Library, where he also liked to hang out, called 'Anatomy for the Artist' written by the author Woolf. Therein he learnt about various muscles in the nose area: Compressor, Dilator, Elevator, Alae and Nasal, Muscles. These controlled ascending, etc. processes around the nasal area. His study into the structure of the nose led him to start his 'nose yoga'.

Michael believed that if you keep exercising the nose, moving it about enough, similar to twitching it, it could keep one protected from getting colds! Michael recommended, for example, practising nose yoga for half an hour daily. This might not only help with one's health, he said, it could also strengthen the nose.

Michael mentioned the lyrics of the song 'The Way You Look Tonight' which includes a repeated line 'And that laugh that wrinkles your nose' Michael demonstrated wrinkling his nose, and it was quite funny to see.

All that twitching of the nose is indeed quite strange, so possibly best to do it in private! Check it out by looking in the mirror! Incidentally, looking in the mirror, itself could be a multi-layered metaphor for Self-Enquiry.

A helpful question one might pose is, who or what is being seen and who indeed or what is seeing it? This may help the leap into the deep end of the Ocean of 'who I really am.' I might just be a fish! When you burst out laughing, you probably have got it. Until you haven't!

3. See Moich Abrahams artwork by visiting his older website - www.moichabrahams.co.uk .
Alternatively, see Moich's art works by visiting his new upcoming website - wwwmoichcreations.com.
For a direct viewing of the piece called 'Two Heads' go to - https://tinyurl.com/kbccs6nj. One of the most interesting paradoxes is that it is impossible to talk or write about Non-Duality

CHAPTER 11 - SPIRITUAL CRISIS & REALISATION

meaningfully. Almost any description used is false and misleading. So visual art is a perfect way to explore the topic of 'Who am I'?

Chapter 12

Becoming an urban hermit[1]

"Just being... in the world but not of it."

Sufi quote

Michael habitually had various familiar places or 'stations' to stand, sit and merge for hours with what is. Though somewhat like a feature, a lamp post perhaps, he is mainly unnoticed by most people hurrying by. Sort of invisible in plain sight.

I often wondered why swarms of little flying insects, like gnats or midges, seem to circle around concentrated in just one spot, instead of dispersing all over the place. I believe it is something to do with the male insect's sexual behaviour to attract a female mate. I don't think that was Michael's reason.

Similarly, I also wondered why Michael is fixated or fixed, or so attached to his familiar haunt of Lavender

CHAPTER 12: BECOMING AN URBAN HERMIT

Hill and Clapham Junction in Battersea. Why Battersea? Why not Chelsea? Haunt is the appropriate word indeed, for there were key people, important 'ghosts' in Michael's life, who also had a strong Battersea connection. From what I gathered, his real mother and her third husband ended up living nearby. Could there be a Freudian connection here? Michael's stepfather, who was his real mum's third husband, is recorded to have died in Battersea. Then there was Michael's very special 'friend-girl', Nell Dunn. Despite being from an aristocratic background, she spent quite some time working in a factory in Battersea and then wrote her famous story for the film Up the Junction about working-class life in Clapham Junction. Also, one of Michael's favourite musicians, 'blind' George Shearing, was born in Battersea.

A favourite place where Michael liked to hang out was near the Lavender Hill Post office outside the huge Asdasupermarket.

There is a little patio area where Michael would come and share his sandwich lunch with a flock of waiting pigeons and the more assertive rooks.

If I had enough money, and if the council allowed it, I would organise a life-size bronze statue of Michael, just like in the photo, feeding the pigeons and rooks placed there doing just that. A little reminiscent of St Francis, perhaps. Anyone up for financing me to do that?

There's a lady there who also came to feed the pigeons. I've seen her there on several occasions feeding them in the same patch. Michael and the lady rarely talk. She has bright red hair.

Life as a 'street person

Whilst with Michael, in the summer of COVID, I oft kept him company, sitting on the wide window ledge, which sort of sufficed as seat and table for our bits and bobs and takeaway lunch outside HSBC in Lavender Hill. On one occasion, I was chatting with another passing regular habitue of the street, who had come to greet us. I sometimes did this, being a friendly person. Michael would rarely join in the conversation, other than an affirmative grunt or so.

Whilst chatting like this, somebody else passing by called out, "Get a job!" Was that addressed to me or one of the other two? With reference to the chap I was chatting to, probably foolishly, I impetuously replied, "He has a job, begging in Asda," which is actually how this other fellow mostly spends his time. "You are overqualified to get a job!" I jested to him. "Too much

CHAPTER 12: BECOMING AN URBAN HERMIT

spitting," Michael commented, possibly referring to the hostile exchange with the stranger.

Michael didn't like technology. He didn't even like to use a cash machine when he needed money and usually asked me to assist him, using his card in the machine. When I tried to teach him the process, step by step, he said that he doesn't really want to know. After getting the money from the cash machine, one time I 'd left him on his own for a bit. When I got back, he seemed a little stressed, having one of those conversations or arguments with himself, with accompanying gestures.

Michael never wanted to kill any life forms... and wherever he saw a very small creature, referring to it as a micro- organism, he'd take excessive care not to disturb it. Unfortunately, Michael became a victim of his own unworldliness; allowing his flat in Connor Court to become overrun with mice, which of course, he wouldn't harm.

He became sick and didn't eat for ten days and ended up in hospital in the 'Observation and Care Ward'. Perhaps Michael's caring about the mice made his situation somewhat similar to the story[2] of the Buddha, who, in a previous incarnation, was a compassionate hare.

The summer of 2020, sometimes was very warm, in fact, blazing hot for quite a few weeks. Michael rarely changed his clothes at that time. He had been sitting in that summer sun, either still with his heavy winter jacket on or having it on his lap and wearing nothing above the waist, baring his skeletal chest for all to see. I bought him a shirt - it was a brown and cream batik made in Indonesia with interesting exotic bird motif designs all over it in a sort of aboriginal style. He looked good in it. I said, "Clothes maketh the man. What do you think of that?"

Michael replied, "Good manners maketh the man." "Oh, yes, but what about the other statement?" I replied.

"Oh, yes," he said, adding the "maybe," word Michael often uses. I said to him that now people could mistake him for an ordinary bloke. "A huge mistake," commented Michael.

To most people passing by, Michael may have seemed like an eccentric and a down-and-out street person. Others simply do not see him, though there he was, in plain sight. Their preoccupied gaze is probably mostly inwards and focused on their own thoughts and concerns.

As the hub for the huge Clapham Junction Railway station, this area called Clapham Junction is a mecca for various down and outs, some selling 'The Big Issue'. This is a magazine produced for the homeless to sell so that they could afford a night in sheltered accommodation. All descriptions of beggars and pseudo beggars congregate here, and one or two odd souls like Michael. Some tend to accost every passerby for small change.

CHAPTER 12: BECOMING AN URBAN HERMIT

It must be said clearly that although Michael seems to have very little money, primarily just what the National Benefit Allowance gives him, and although he may look like one, he is definitely not a beggar. On the contrary, one of the most enlightening things I have witnessed about Michael is that he is regularly approached by some of these local characters, who seem to know him, and vice versa, who come up to him for a small 'handout' which he gives without question, from his modest pension.

They initially enquire, "How are you, Michael", that being the prologue for Michael to dig deep into his pocket and give them a pound or two, enough for a hot cup of tea or coffee. I've seen this routine enacted on many occasions. It seems that they can count on Michael to be a 'soft touch'.

Often he didn't mind me taking photographs of him. Indeed, sometimes he would pose. Perhaps I'd ask him to hold my phone or the small handheld Orangina music speaker device as if using or listening to some music. However, sometimes he definitely didn't want to be photographed and covered his face with his hands.

Michael has occasionally been connected with various social workers, as you may expect if you appeared to be a 'street person.' "A social worker, called Yvonne, gave me her mother's raincoat", said Michael. He added the fact that Yvonne's mother was an artist.

Another social services Mental Health Care experience

which Michael recounted related to Tooting Bec Hospital.

He said he was approximately 50 at the time. He mentioned a Jamaican social worker, called Joya. "She 'got me' into a place (in the hospital) which was looked after by a lady called Joyce." There were only male residents there."Michael said. "It was for 'Patient After Care' - should we say psychological". Michael then added dismissively. "I stayed in the hospital... to live there for a while; that's all it was". After that, Michael said, he went off on his own, to live somewhere in Tooting Bec.

Footnotes:

1. cf. A Pelican in the Wilderness; subtitle: Hermits, solitaries and recluses by Isabel Colegate, Harper Collins. This includes stories about many interesting characters, such as Howard Hughes and Sri Ramana Maharshi.

2. A Fable. In a previous reincarnation, Buddha was a hare. Hopping along, the hare saw a man sitting by a log fire. The man looked starving, having not eaten for many days. The hare had compassion for the man and leapt into the fire to provide himself as food for the man. This fable is commemorated in Asia by images of a hare on the moon, and children are taught to look up at the full moon to see the hare, as a previous reincarnation of the Buddha, who demonstrated his great compassion by sacrificing himself. Regarding Michael and the mice, if

CHAPTER 12: BECOMING AN URBAN HERMIT

you look up at the full moon in the future, you may see this unworldly man there.

Chapter 13

Photos of Michael
(around Clapham Junction and Lavender Hill)

"One who lives in his real being takes himself for nothing."

Jean Klein

CHAPTER 13: PHOTOS OF MICHAEL

Outside HSBC

www.moichcreations.com

Near Asda in a favourite spot

CHAPTER 13: PHOTOS OF MICHAEL

Having a simple lunch

Michael reading an interesting little booklet

CHAPTER 13: PHOTOS OF MICHAEL

Michael enjoying carrot cake outside the post office.

www.moichcreations.com

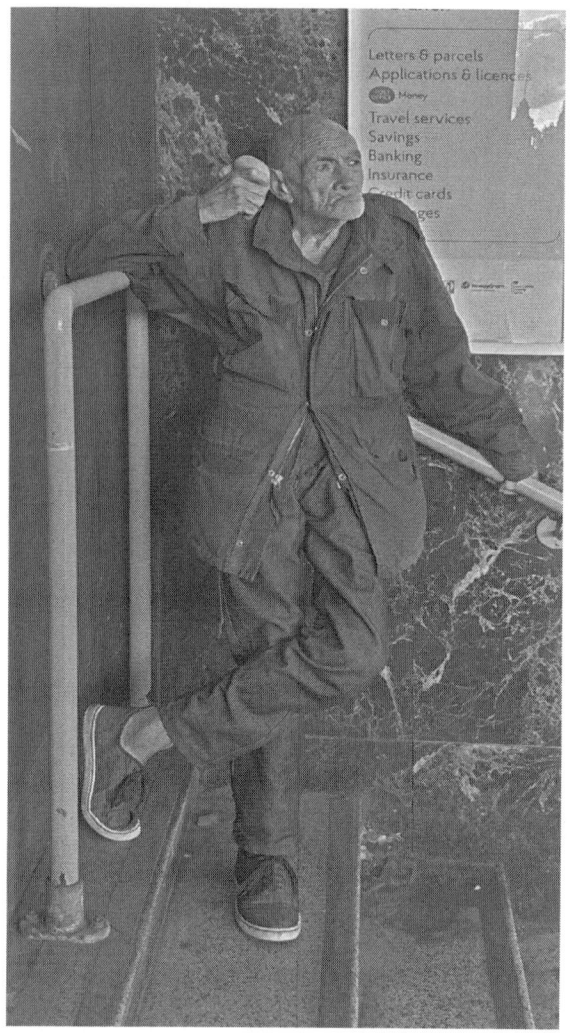

Sheltering from the rain outside the post office whilst listening to his favourite tunes.

To see these photos of Michael, and some others, in full colour, visit my upcoming website at www.moichcreations.com

Chapter 14

Friends & Hangouts

"Walk in life without any pockets. Don't keep anything."

Mooji

The Art Connection

As mentioned earlier, the relationship between Michael and me initially took off because of our art connection. This stems from Michael's love of looking at art, which began when he was young and studied art and Moich'spassion as a practising artist.

As our friendship continued, as always, art remained the catalyst for many interesting chats.

You are invited to explore Moich's art via www.MoichCreations.com

The grocers shop

One place where Michael used to 'hang out' in his earlier years was in a grocer's shop run by a Greek lady named

CHAPTER 14 - FRIENDS & HANGOUTS

Antigone. She allowed Michael to stay in her shop reading the newspaper; she was also an artist and sympathised with his 'situation'.

Michael lived nearby and he said he went there for his 'victuals.' They eventually sold the store, but Antigone's mother, Georgina, continued to work there. Antigone later worked in an Art Gallery in Putney and married a half-Greek, half-English guy called George.

Michael and his barber

During the time of the Covid Pandemic, visiting a barber was banned and illegal. It was deemed so because of potential interactions with Covid carriers. Michael being elderly and having secondary health symptoms such asserious asthma and possible kidney infection, and having low immunity made him vulnerable.

Michael usually visited a young Turkish barber in Lavender Hill. Despite the new Covid regulations, forbidding such activities, Michael obstinately resorted to his habitual visit there. He told me that recently the guy had taken him into a darkened back room to do the deed, of course, because it was illegal.

These visits to the barber used to happen when the young Turkish chap saw Michael in the street; he rushed out, telling him to come for a haircut and a shave which actually amounts to nothing more than a close trim of his beard. Michael told me that he paid a rather exorbitant amount for this service.

I had been used to giving myself a hair trim during the time when the government had banned visiting hairdressers. I'd bought myself exactly the same hairdresser tool that the hairdressers use in their salon.

When Michael first moved to his new home (see Chapter 16), to celebrate, I also bought one for Michael. More hygienic to have his own. I was legally allowed to be closeto Michael as his 'bubble ' person.

Using this new apparatus, I offered to trim his hair, to which he agreed, and also gave him, it turned out to be one time only, a really good, proper close shave. Michael looked so much younger after that. This was probably the first time in many years that he actually had a shave rather than a trim.

Michael has a sort of special interest in Turkish people. He used to know a young woman, also called Monika, whose Turkish boyfriend worked in another cafe that Michael used to frequent in the noughties (2000 - 2010) in Wandsworth, called 'Westies', which no longer exists. Michael was very fond of that lady. He said that she used to be very kind to him, persuading her boyfriend to allow Michael to sit in that cafe for hours.

When Westies was closing, they told Michael about a new cafe in Clapham Junction called Jacks, which then

CHAPTER 14 - FRIENDS & HANGOUTS

became one of Michael's regular haunts.

Also, prior to the young Turkish boy barber, from Lavender Hill, there was a young female Turkish barber who used to cut or trim Michael's hair and beard. These Turkish connections clearly had become important to Michael. He said to me that he wants to "keep in with the Turkish", declining when I offered to cut it again for him. I think that the earlier associations with Turkish people was why he accepted the pressured invitation from the young barber.

One time, while suggesting that I could cut his hair and shave him again properly, he insisted to me that he wanted to go to the Turkish fellow. "I need to stay on good terms with the Turkish," he said.

Michael once said, again in his enigmatic way, "The air is better than the hair because the roots are truly gone. The air on the roots of the hair is better than the hair on the roots of the hair." He went on, "Is the hair lying?" Did he simply mean that before he had a haircut, the hair covered the roots of the hair, and the air couldn't get to the roots? In order for the air to get to the roots, he needed a haircut. Or was there a deeper meaning, the roots referring to something else?

Michael loved connecting ideas. After reading the daily newspaper, which he enjoyed doing, he made an initially obscure comment that "the 'Instructive System' collapses when reading the newspaper. It's all about the way the world is". I think Michael may have been referring to Ouspensky's Fourth Way, which taught about how to wake up from this worldly dream which gets forgotten when one spends time following the usually rehashed and often depressing news. As it is said, where the mind goes, the energy flows. "Not everything is bad news," Michael said, "so to speak". For example, he said, "The scientists discovered the Covid vaccine."

Maddie and me... the beginnings of the 'dream team' at KFC

In about 2017, Michael told me that he had met a lady called Maddie and was meeting her in KFC ('Kentucky Fried Chicken'). He told me I would be welcome to join them. I was intrigued. This, apparently, was a fairly regular rendezvous, but I didn't want to intrude. Michael repeatedly invited me to join them, and eventually, I accepted his invitation.

Maddie turned out to be a very pleasant young lady, in her twenties, who had come across Michael in one of his regular spots. After talking to him, she decided to make a habit of checking up on him to see that he was okay and, in fact, to befriend him. A wonderful noble gesture. What a lucky old man! Her mother was a social worker, so it appeared that she had this caring streak in her genes. The three of us started to meet fairly regularly in KFC, and Maddie and I became friends too. KFC became one of Michael's favourite 'resting' places, especially when the weather was inclement, and I'd occasionally join him there. When the weather was fine, he'd prefer to be outside, often somewhere near the pigeons and crows; as shown in the photographs.

Debenhams

As winter approached, after finding him standing, in one of his regular spots, in all weathers, or sheltering in a bus stop, I encouraged Michael to go with me into a warmer place. A great place nearby was Debenhams, the local superstore with an inviting and warm cafe upstairs, on the top floor. Sadly, that store has now closed. It was a great cafe which seemed to be a favourite of older people seeking a genteel, warm and quiet environment to while away hours reading their free copy of Metro or chatting with their friends. It had a wonderful large art nouveau stained glass concave window above the seating area that gave the place a real sense of timeless character.

Sadly, in the summer of 2020, perhaps because of Covid, Debenhams closed this branch. Its frontage has been boarded up ever since. There may be a plan to turn it into offices so it looks likely that our wonderful place of relaxation and refreshment, away from the street, will be no more. As Buddha pointed out, as one of the three marks or stains of existence, all things are subject to change... the law of impermanence (anicca, Sanskrit)[2]

Greggs

Greggs became the next big favourite hangout. Michael loves to go there to have a coffee and a sausage roll, sometimes a tomato soup. Several workers there knew him very well and allowed him to stay inside, sheltered from the rain.

On occasion, Michael asked me to meet him to help him use the cash machine at Lloyds, which was near Greggs, as he didn't like to do it himself.

Michael often used to stand there, just outside Greggs, near the bus stop, somewhat like a lamp post, making it his regular spot for hours, before moving up to Lavender Hill to spend time with the pigeons.

Sometimes, there were people nearby, jogging along the high street. One obsession Michel had was about being accused of pick pocketing. He said, "Every time these runners," probably referring to the men, "bumped into me in the street, I am in prison." He often talked about a certain mysterious lady policewoman', who, if she was there, he said, "would keep an eye on 'things'". The topic of stealing, or theft, whether, fictitiously, by Michael or from him, was often alluded to; clearly something he was anxious about.

CHAPTER 14 - FRIENDS & HANGOUTS

Cafe Olé

Cafe Olé is another café or restaurant that I introduced him to. It's right next to the new Travel Lodge Apartment Hotel, opposite Clapham Junction station.

They have a comfortable sitting area with a very large table at the back of the restaurant, and so felt more private, which Michael preferred. We went there quite often, and the friendly staff began to get used to us.

Jacks

Jacks in Lavender Hill was the cafe that had been recommended by the couple from Westies. It became a very firm favourite either for a takeaway sandwich or to sit inside and have a meal. When we were out resting on the low brick wall near Asda, being entertained by the pigeons, or perching on the nearby large flat window shelf of HSBC, I regularly used to go to get Michael his second or third cup of tea from Jacks.

A takeaway sandwich was often our staple lunch from Jack's. Michael enjoys a sandwich with scrambled eggs, which would be easy for him to chew since he is almost toothless. Washed down with a cup of tea, perhaps with a biscuit.

Talking about dipping biscuits into tea, Michael said, "It's a very old chestnut but an interesting one." Michael liked to make the biscuit soft enough to eat, by dipping it in his tea. He continued. "You have to be careful it doesn't drop into the tea." I said, "You know your biscuits." He replied, "I know my biscuits."

Michael would invariably give half of his sandwich to the pigeons and crows outside. Also, as a dessert, it became a habit to buy a piece of Jacks delicious carrot cake to share. He always insisted on being given only "a fraction", as he said he couldn't eat more, but he did seem to like it.

One day I decided that, since Michael barely ate anything of the carrot cake and the majority that I

CHAPTER 14 - FRIENDS & HANGOUTS

consumed was adding to my own waistline, I should stop buying it. It was very delicious but didn't help me in my wish to lose a bitof my tummy fat.

I told Michael that I would be stopping buying it from then on. Michael said, "Actually, I'm not a carrot cake man". I commented, "Now, after all this time, you are telling me!" Michael replied, "I mustn't make too much of identification". By this I think he is referring to attachment.

The patio outside Asda

During the summer, we sat near these cafes.

Often on a low brick wall which is on the sides of a small patio where Michael loved to feed the pigeons and the crows. He usually gave them about half his lunch which was actually just one sandwich he had just bought from Jack's just down the hill. Probably that's why he looked so skinny.

Michael asked me if the pigeons recognised him, and I said, "Yes… because you feed them nearly every day, but their level of awareness is very low, very basic, and their response is like 'operant conditioning'". Michael then said, "We can only hope to become conscious beings if we use the 'right way'. The energy which is normally used is used the wrong way. Arms straight up. It's about negative emotions and their brahmsamation." Sounds like Brahma and transformation combined? Perhaps Transformation, as Ouspenski used to talk about it? Anyway, he lost me there!

Sitting on that rather uncomfortable low wall, Michael seemed to be meditating. He'd often read the local free daily newspapers, such as the London Metro and Evening Standard, to keep up with the news. I sometimes got him the latter when I visited him in the street in the late afternoon to share a cup of tea and some friendly banter.

He also very much enjoys books or magazines on art, which occasionally, I would bring for him to read; magazines such as Royal Academy Members magazine. After he studied it for quite a while, I asked him, "Did you like it?" he commented, "there's just too much", or "yes, wonderful!"

He sometimes suggested that he knew someone mentionedin the magazine, like John Craxton. Also, this is how I came to learn about the first winner of the Turner Prize, Malcolm Morley, who painted ships and aeroplanes, amongst other things. I looked Malcolm Morley up and found his career quite interesting.

The Ice Cream Parlour

Michael sometimes asked me to help him use the cash machine at Lloyds near Greggs as he didn't like to do it himself. We would go for ice cream afterwards. They were offering everything at half price for a while which meant the

CHAPTER 14 - FRIENDS & HANGOUTS

ice creams seemed to taste even better! After we visited the ice-cream shop, Michael said "Top-Hole", which means excellent, first rate. This British expression, which probably predates WW1, could originate from the British game of Cribbage, where scoring is shown by moving small pegs around a multi-holed board, a game Michael learnt to play in his boarding school days.

Lavender Hill Library

When it was open, Michael would spend ages in the library, enjoying browsing art books. He also had a special interest in books that covered anatomy, with a particular focus on the nose!

Boots the Chemist

I accompanied Michael to Boots, where he would buy his favourite cough sweets, Jakemans, the yellow variety. The manageress Nadia, who knew him well, always paid him special attention, and struck up a conversation with him, asking how he was. Pointing at me, she asked him, "Is that your friend?" Michael replied, "He certainly is," which was gratifying to hear.

She said, "We have known Michael for the last three years. He is a very humble and kind man. He regularly comes into the store, and when he is in a good mood, he chats with us. He never complains about anything and claims he has got no problem. Everyone misses him if he doesn't come into the shop".

Footnotes:

1. The Dream Team. See chapter 16

2. Sanskrit: Three Stains of Existence - Impermanence, Suffering and No-Self. These are some of the foundation concepts that the Buddha taught so that people could find a pathway to real happiness.

Chapter 15

Songs & Literature

"But only art and music have the power to bring peace."
Yoko Ono

When visiting or hanging out with Michael, sometimes I'd look for some of his favourite songs on my mobile phone, which he'd asked for.

Then I'd give him the phone to hold near his good left ear so he could listen to it. He loved this.

One time his special friend Maddie kindly presented me with a fantastic little speaker, a light blue device named 'Orangina'. Made in China, it was small enough to hold in the palm of your hand and could, via Bluetooth, pick up the songs selected on my mobile. This became more practical than passing Michael my mobile phone as Michael could hold this device near his head as I added songs via my mobile from a distance. Listening to Michael's favourite songs became de rigueur as part of ourtime together and happened whenever Michael

CHAPTER 15 - SONGS & LITERATURE

suggested, "Shall we have a song?"

I found that he liked a very specific type of music, mostly songs and tunes from the late 1940s or 1950s, the era of his youth. He enjoys this very much and could be very sentimental when he listens to those tunes expressing his delight by saying "wonderful, wonderful" at the end of the song. On rare occasions, Michael listened to jazz and becomes very animated, even appearing to sort of 'taste' the music by wiggling his tongue. He told me that in his apartment, he would practise daily on an electric piano keyboard[1], practising pieces he knows but without making a sound. The sound was switched off as he didn't like to disturb the people living above him, he said.

He also has a radio and disc player, which he bought from the now defunct Woolworths, and a small collection of about eight cassettes. His all-time favourite song is 'Nina Never Knew' sung by Vic Damone. This is played by far the most times upon request. I once asked Michael if he ever knew anyone called Nina, and that was when the story about a friendship with a Nina in his twenties, came to light.

Nina was indeed a special 'friend-girl', as he refers to the ladies he has known. As mentioned, previously, I asked if that friendship had anything to do with this being Michael's favourite song, but he responded, "Oh, no, just a friend-girl". I suspect Michael had feelings for her that he preferred not to express. As Michael liked that song so much and asked me to play this song so often to him, I have added the lyrics of 'Nina Never Knew' here:

> Girls were made to kiss, but Nina never knew;
> Girls are born for this, but Nina never knew;
> Sweet surprise filled Nina's eyes.
>
> She did not understand when I kissed her hand.
> Why dreams began to stir deep down inside of her;
> When I whispered things that Nina never heard.
> Nina's heart took wings with ev'ry tender word.
> Then suddenly, she clung to me;
> She learned to love somehow.
> And I'm so glad that Nina never knew till now.
>
> Songwriters: Louis Alter / Milton Drake

One of Michael's favourite musicians was George Shearing (1919 - 2011). He was born in Battersea and was blind from birth. Whenever mentioning one of George Shearing's songs, Michael would say 'Blind Battersea'. Incidentally, there is now a George Shearing Centre in Battersea, opened to provide facilities for disabled people. George was the youngest of nine children, born into a poor, working-class family.

His father delivered coal, and his mother cleaned trains for a living. He emigrated to America in 1947 and created the world-famous George Shearing Quintet sound in 1949. George was invited by three US Presidents (Ford, Carter and Reagan) to play at the White House and was knighted by the Queen in 2007.

CHAPTER 15 - SONGS & LITERATURE

Not bad for a Battersea boy! Another favourite George Shearing song was Canadian Sunset[2], with music by jazz pianist Eddie Heywood and lyrics by Norman Gimbel. It was high up on the charts in 1956 when Michael was 23.

Other songs by George Shearing:

- Early Autumn
- Night and Day
- Tenderly, also sung by Billie Holiday
- Star Eyes, also by Beryl Davis
- Poinciana (Song of a Tree) with music by Nat Simon and lyrics by Buddy Bernier and Manhattan Transfer from the Early years Album (Jazz and Blues). Poinciana was another of Michael's all-time most requested songs.

More of Michael's favourite singers and songs he asked to have played to him include:

Songs by Johnnie Ray:

- A Sinner Am I - this song is another absolute all-time favourite of Michael
- Please, Mr Sun
- Glad Rag Doll
- Hey There
- Look, Homeward Angel
- If You Believe
- Somebody Stole My Gal

Songs by Frank Sinatra:
- There's No You
- There's a small hotel
- You're Sensational
- Laura
- Take Me, with Tommy Dorsey and his orchestra

Songs by Cole Porter:
- Dancing cheek to cheek
- I have got you under my skin or by Julie London
- Begin the Beguine or by Artie Shaw

Songs by Julie London:
- Black Coffee
- What Can I say

Songs by the Four Freshman:
- Shangri La - another Michael frequently requested.
- You stepped Out of a Dream, also by Sarah Vaughan

More favourites, mainly from that era, include:

- Cheek to cheek by Fred Astaire
- Piano solo by Ebbs Tide
- Laura by Charlie Parker
- At Last by Glenn Miller
- Ebb Tide by The Platters
- Serenata by Sarah Vaughan
- Flamingo by Carmen Mcrae
- On the Road by Vic Damone

CHAPTER 15 - SONGS & LITERATURE

- A Sleepy Lagoon by Doris Day
- Pretty Flamingo by Mark Barkan
- Bluebirds in the Moonlight by Beryl Davis
- Dangerous Moonlight by Anton Walbrook
- Venus by Jonny Osmond, Frankie Avalon
- Lost in a Hot Summer Night by June Christy
- 'Isn't it Romantic?' by Lorenz Hart and Richard Rogers
- Walking Back To Happiness by Helen Shapiro, Music by Irving Berlin, Stephane Grappelli and Andre Previn
- Blue Malibu, "I want to be conscious of 'Blue Malibu", said Michael.
- Moonlight in Vermont by Ella Fitzgerald and Louis Armstrong
- Love of My Life by Judy Garland I like to roam around lazy countryside
- Ac-Cent-Tchu-Ate The Positive, Eliminate the negative" Andrew Sisters
- Can't by Mel Torme, ('Til that lucky day, you know darn well, I can't give you anything but love baby)
- On a little street in Singapore 1940 by Ray Eberle, or Manhattan Transfer. A top favourite.
- Autumn Serenade by Johnny Hartman with John or Eddie, or Coltrane. "An awesome song" commented Michael; on hearing this, he exclaimed; "Wonderful!" It could be incredibly terrible, but it is incredibly wonderful![3]

- In other words, Fly me to the moon, and The nearness of you by Nancy Wilson; (Michael was listening to this with his arm raised. He said he thought it helped his asthma.)
- I've got to be getting along by Stan Kenton, band leader, composer and pianist. Michael once said, "I've got to be getting along or something, in the words of Stan Kenton."

Michael said, "How long can you stay?" Having no plan, I replied, "How long is a piece of string?" Michael then asked, " Could we listen to 'I've Got The World On a String' (Mel Torme)", so we played it.

Michael would usually tell me to turn the volume of the little Orangina speaker device down, saying, "We don't want to be mistaken for Bohemians!"

He liked to practise on his keyboard for at least an hour a day. In his previous flat, he used to do this in silence. He didn't actually press any keys so as not to disturb those living upstairs or downstairs. "Practise every day gives my life some cohesion," he said. Michael even keeps the volume down in his new flat, when practising on his keyboard, and if I suggested otherwise, he would remind me that he wasn't a Bohemian, "We wouldn't want to join the Bohemian Club." Michael seemed to associate the word bohemian with being loud; however, Michael said the phrase about being Bohemian was an

CHAPTER 15 - SONGS & LITERATURE

invention of his friend, author Lady Antonia Fraser. About making a noise, Michael always turns his radio off at 10 pm, citing that he didn't want to be a bother to anyone.

Michael's favourite artists and paintings.

Talking about his art in his 20s, Michael said, "The paintings I did at that time, were all sketches of coffee pots and mugs, and they all sold." I asked, "You must have admired Morandi?" and he replied, "Yes, I think his paintings were wonderful."

Michael liked to tell me about artists who played an instrument. "Paul Klee was a professional violinist. Paul pronounced Pawl," emphasised Michael. "Gauguin played the piano and double bass. Douanier Rousseau played a small piano keyboard, although it was not electric like my one. Michael mentioned that somebody played the harmonium in one of Matisse's paintings. I ought to go to Czechoslovakia," said Michael. "Why?" I asked. "To check everything!" (Czech - check), his play on words, referring to checking who played which instrument.

One day Michael asked me what artists influenced me. After answering, I asked him the same question. He said, "If I am blessed to live longer, I'll have to think about which ones could influence me in the future." Later I questioned him as to what he preferred, music or art. "Both" he replied.

Then Michael threw into the conversation the Spanish name

Olvidados referring to the Spanish film 'Los Olvidados'. This was known in the US as The Young and the Damned, which is a film directed by Buñuel made in 1950; when Michael would have been about 17.

Michael had previously expressed interest in works by Buñuel and Dali and also spoke of Braque. Michael said the name Braque translated means - grey beard. Michael discovered this when he was studying a book of Braque's drawings called 'Illustrated Notebooks. 1917-1955 translated by Stanley Appel-baum. Collections of Fine Art, Dover Publications 1971.' This book usually sat next to his keyboard.

Since they are rather thought-provoking, here are a few quotes by Braque from that book.

'Nature doesn't give you a taste for perfection. You can't conceive of it as being better or worse than it is.'

'We will never have repose. The present is perpetual!'

'Art is meant to upset people. Science reassures them.'

'You should not imitate what you want to create.'

'In Art, there is only one thing that counts, the thing you can't explain.'

'Those who lead the way, turn their back on their followers. That is just what the followers deserve.'

'I like the rule which corrects emotion.'

CHAPTER 15 - SONGS & LITERATURE

'Art soars above things; science gives you crutches.'

'I am much more interested in achieving unison with Nature than in copying it.'

'For every acquisition, there is an equivalent loss. That is the Law of Compensation.'

'Limited means produce new forms, inspires creativity, makes a style. Progress in Art does not consist in reducing limitations, but in knowing them better.'

In another conversation I had with Michael about film, he came out with some snippets about the film star Kirk Douglas. Michael said that Douglas had four sons, as mentioned, in Douglas' biography entitled 'The Ragman's Son'. Michael then went on to talk about how wonderful Kirk Douglas was in the film 'Lust for Life' as Vincent van Gogh. Michael then mentioned that Vincent was buried next to his brother Theo. That comment may have been prompted by the fact that earlier, I had confided that I had made arrangements for my own brother to be buried in the plot adjacent to mine!

Michael sometimes referred to a connection between the music of Vic Damone and Lichtenstein's art. He said that Lichtenstein's art is very similar to the lyrics of Nina Never Knew. I told Michael that I was puzzled by that. (and still am unless it somehow means all things are equal when one is not attached) .Michael retorted, "Stop worrying and start living." adding, "I heard that (phrase) from Elsie, an Indian girl."I sometimes lightly call Michael, 'Master, Boss or Guv'. He commented that Juan Gris, the painter used to call Picasso, 'Master'- and Gertrude Stein observed that Picasso didn't like that. Picasso painted a great portrait of her early on in his career. Picasso was a wonderful painter, Michael said.

Michael loved using his languages, and often quoted in Latin "Pax Lex", meaning Peace Law, as an important principle to remember. Michael said, *"If artists are not peace-loving, they are not really artists"*

What follows is a bit like a kaleidoscope taking a literary rollercoaster.

Henrik Ibsen

A curious conversation arose about Henrik Ibsen. Michael asked me, "And how are you today?" I playfully replied, using one of Michaels own responses, "Consciousness shining". Michael said he liked that. Then he artfully again repeated, 'And how are you today?' this time telling me that he was quoting from the play 'An Enemy of the People' written by Henrik Ibsen. He then quoted, from the same play, "That goes without saying". Michael had a good memory.

"Ibsen was into politics," Michael said, "and he had something to do with Suez." Michael then instructed me to check this fact. Michael was spot on, as it turned out that Ibsen had attended the opening of the Suez Canal in 1869on an invitation from the Swedish King. Ibsen's long poem 'Peer Gynt' (yes, poem!) takes the unfaithful Norwegian national character to Egypt as well. Here Peer meets first the Bedouin girl Anitra in the desert and later the representatives of the European political landscape - in a madhouse* in Cairo (*Ibsen's phrasing).

Michael has a thing about not drinking alcohol, it might be a health thing, but it could also be part of his spirituality and protecting his 'consciousness shining'. Michael quoted the line 'I never indulge in spirits' from Act II of the Ibsen play 'An Enemy of the People'.

On another occasion, rambling on as he does from time to time, Michael said that Anne Brontë was criticised by her sister Charlotte regarding the work 'The Tenant of Wild Fell Hall', 1800.

James Hadley Chase

Then, jumping about in this conversation, Michael said, 'That's the way the cookie crumbles'. This is the title of a book written by James Hadley Chase. He said that it was a wonderful book. Michael said he had read seventy of James Hadley Chase's books! He had got these from the library. "Are you a member of the library? I asked. "Oh! Definitely!" he replied. Michael said that George Orwell wrote a favourable review of James Hadley Chase's 'That's How the Cookie Crumbles'. 'You are Dead without Money' was another book by Chase. Michael commented on that title, saying, "Without money, you could not feed the pigeons." Michael, as he does, adds a piece of memory flotsam, floating up in his mind, saying, "I recall some chap getting on a train carrying a paperback book, by James Hadley Chase".

Chase was one of the best-known thriller writers of all time. His canon, comprising 90 titles, earned him a reputation as the king of thriller writers in Europe. He was also one of the internationally best-selling authors, and to date, 50 of his books have been made into films.

Another time referring again to that phrase, that consciousness is nowadays used in the 'wrong way, Michael said, "To achieve transformation, the right way is to grab a fistful of clouds or something. That's a different 'something' from Francis Bacon's cup of tea or something. The wrong way is to reach for a gun, of course," Michael said. Although it was referred to earlier that, for Michael, firing a gun was synonymous with using negative emotions, guns are something Michael has concerns about. We discussed this by comparing it with the right to bear arms as in the USA American 2nd Amendment.

However, I was barking up the wrong tree, and it turned out that Michael was quoting a novel about a so-called Hero who sees himself as a tough kind of detective solving some crime or other.

The phrase "grab a fistful of clouds" turned out coined

from a book by James Hadley Chase. Incidentally, Michael told me that it was not his real name. His real name is Rene Brabiton Raymond. I told Michael that I'd purchased this book online from Amazon, and Michael said that he would then test me on English Literature to see what I'd read.

"I'm Vull," Michael would sometimes say after food. Meaning full up. This expression 'Vull' comes from the book: a Child in the Forest' by Winifred Foley. This was the original title of 'Full hearts and Empty Bellies' - her autobiography about her childhood time in the 1920s in the Forest of Dean... ending up on the streets of London. She died in Cheltenham... another place connected with Michael.

Aldous Huxley

Once, while Michael was having his dinner, he apparently had enough and said, "It's not to say it's not quite eatable." I offered the word, "edible", and Michael, in his inimitable way, enlightened me by referring to Aldous Huxley. "Aldous Huxley used the word eatable." He used it in his book 'After the Fireworks'.[3] Using a kind of poetic licence, Michael said, "'not quite eatable' meaning 'not so desirable'." Michael has also read Aldous Huxley's comic story 'Antique Hay' and his novel 'Point Counter Point'.

Michael also mentioned that Aldous Huxley used the phrase Self-Sculpture. The idea is to have a sense of proportion, Michael said. He then mentioned T.S. Elliot's poetry, something about 'the wind in the high grass.' "There is nothing there at all unless the two forces (male and female) put it together," this time referring to Malraux's 'The Human Condition'.

Les Femmes Savante

Michael had read and often quoted to me from the five-act comedy written in verse, Les Femmes Savante (The Learned Ladies) - a favourite play by Moliere which is a satire on academic pretension, female education, and préciosité (French for preciousness). It was one of Moliere's most popular comedies and premiered at the Théâtre du Palais-Royal on 11 March 1672. Michael quoted Henriette in it, singing to her sister, "...this noeud (marriage knot) doesn't appeal to me".

Michael also referred to a phrase that amused him from another work by Moliere: La Ragout d'un Galant, about ragout or gallant's stew. The term "stew" is used in comic literature to refer to a female sexual appetite. "And to satisfy your greedy appetite, does her husband need a gallant's stew?" The Imaginary Cuckold, (scene VI, verse 171-172). Another time, Michael was reading Moliere in the original French. A play called 'Psyche'. A character called La Contesse might have been the name of a play and also the main protagonist in the play, Contesse Escarbagners. "Why don't we go and see Psyche?" Michael quoted a line from the Play.

CHAPTER 15 - SONGS & LITERATURE

We were talking about his crossword puzzle in the Metro newspaper and the need to weigh up the words, word by word, when Michael, getting into a flow, quoted precisely from Moliere's Les Femmes Savanntes "Mets-nous ici pour écouter à l'aise Ces vers que mot à mot il est besoin qu'on." (My rendering). This translated as..."Let's put ourselves to listen comfortably to these verses word by word and weigh them up" (scales of Justice).

He continued quoting Chrysale in the play, asking "Suis -je un fat , s'il vous plait?" (Am I an idiot?) Molière Act V, scene II. Henriette, Chrysale's daughter, replies "Je ne dis pas cela" (I'm not saying that).

Michael commented, "It absolutely rings a bell with modern speech".

He then went on, "I know a bank where the wild thyme blows... oxlips and the nodding violet grows; quite over-canopied with luscious woodbine, with sweet musk roses, and with eglantine..."from Shakespeare's A Midsummer Night's Dream. "A star of a sonnet", added Michael.

To while away the afternoon, during the rather warm sunny summer days of 2020, as he sat there, in a favourite place, as mentioned, I sometimes brought Michael a book about art to browse through. This time I had two art magazines, and as I offered him the second one, Michael declined, saying: "Multiplicity", referring, of course, to the antithesis of his beloved Unity principle. I replied, "It doesn't exist" Michael, in turn, replied: "Let's hope not". My comment that "multiplicity doesn't exist, just in case you are still following this, is a reference confirming that the Unity principle implies its essence is **indivisible**, hence there can be only one of it. Regarding Michael's further comment, would be him agreeing with that.

We went together into a posh shop nearby called Whole Foods which sells quality organic products. Often the produce there is double the price of other nearby shops like Asda. Michael occasionally likes to buy some cheese and looked in wonder at their amazing selection of produce. Michael is partial to Jarlsberg cheese, so he buys it there.

Michael likes to have three cups of tea in the afternoon. I think he would have drunk more if he could, but his catheter bag wouldn't allow it. "This tea is the bee's knees!" Michael once exclaimed.

I once cautioned Michael to be careful not to get sunstroke... it was so hot that afternoon. He told me not to worry. I replied, 'worry' is not in my vocabulary (I wish that were always the case!). Michael retorted, "it (worry) doesn't exist", with a big grin on his face. "Stop worrying. Start living," said Michael.

Another strange conversation while Michael was looking at a little monograph (a concise publication) showing photographic reproductions of artworks by Miro. I asked Michael which of Miro's paintings he preferred. He said that if he told me that, the other paintings could commit suicide! I replied, "that can't be so because paintings don't have an ego."

"So they can't be bruised by me, only Bruced" (referring to his middle name), he replied with a smile.

These are the sort of books Michael loves:

Leonardo and the Human Body by Leonardo da Vinci; America: A Prophecy, Europe: A Prophecy, and Songs of Innocence by William Blake; Une Semaine de Bonte: A Surrealistic Novel in Collage by Max Ernst; La Tauromaquia and Bulls of Bordeaux and The Disparates (The Proverb) by Francisco Goya; Ecco Homo by Georges Grosz; The Dance of Death by: Hans Holbein the Younger.

Footnotes:

1. Concerning his music, Michael mentioned Dr Jean-Baptiste Lully (1632-1687), who was an Italian-born French composer, instrumentalist, and dancer who spent most of his life working in the court of Louis XIV of France. He is considered a master of the French Baroque style. He wrote a musical 'Monsieur de Pourceaugnac', with Moliere. This famous French playwright was Michael's favourite. He read plays by Moliere in the original French and, as you saw, could quote from them.

2. Michael did a signed and dated 2020 sketch for me that he called a 'drawing' of the tune 'Canadian Sunset' – See a photo of the drawing on page 29 – Chapter 3.

Michael loves this song very much, saying, "It is wonderful, total enlightenment!" He would listen to it with his left foot raised and his right foot tapping the floor. I'm not sure if it was from yoga or excitement. Certainly, one of the 17th-century yoga practices that Michael told me about was to have one foot off the ground.

3. First published one year before he wrote his classic 'Brave New World', 'After the Fireworks' is Aldous Huxley at the height of his powers. (1926).

Chapter 16

Satsang[1] with Michael

"Deep inside of you is a 'Guru' with the wisdom of the entire Universe"

Gurudev Sri Sri Ravi Shankar

Alan Wilson Watts wrote

"Jesus Christ knew he was God. So, wake up and find out eventually who you really are. In our culture, of course, if you announce something similar, they'll say you're crazy, and you're blasphemous, and they'll either put you in jail or in a nuthouse (which is pretty much the same thing).

However, if you wake up in India and tell your friends and relations, 'My goodness, I've just discovered that I'm God,' they'll laugh and say, 'Oh, congratulations, at last, you found out'."

(The Essential Alan Watts)

CHAPTER 16 - SATSANG WITH MICHAEL

What follows are Michael's responses to the author's questions and dialogue on being awake, Union with God and Self-enquiry. Often perplexing to follow.

These strange insights didn't happen all on one occasion, they took place over a period between 2019 and 2022.

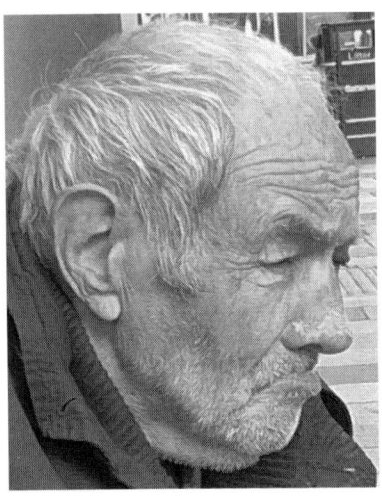

Q: What is the meaning of Life?
A: "Daily life is Divinity."

Sometimes we had a funny little banter.

Michael said, "Zen is interesting; utterly interesting." I said, "It's so interesting that it is totally uninteresting.

"That's true," Michael replied. "I can't make myself somebody because I am a nobody," said Michael. Then referring to his friend Jeze, as he often did, from his time sixty years earlier in Paris, he said, "But you are assisting my friend Jeze, dead or alive." "How?" I asked. "On being a nobody - Being a friend to me is important, more because of Jeze rather than me. When the body dies, the soul leaves the navel and travels to the void. When in the void, they are all nobodies."

Reflecting, I thought, we are not alive for a very, very long time, before and after our short time alive. So essentially, most of the time, infinite time, we are nobodies. These strange ideas are a bit existential, which is probably why Michael mentioned the famous Existentialist author, Jean-Paul Sartre. "I did see him in Montmartre buying stamps," said Michael.

Michael continued:

"It's a very rare achievement being a 'nobody', that is, to overcome the ego in one's lifetime. But up in the void, they are all like that."

"Have they got a sense of self?" I asked.

"The soul is still conscious," replied Michael.

Then I told Michael about the Zen story of a new student where the Zen Master asked the student, "What is Zen?" and the student replied, "I don't know." The student then asked the Zen Master, "So what is Zen?" The Master replied, "I don't know."

Michael commented, "This is about two levels of knowing." (The Master's level and the student's level.)

Then Michael quoted the famous Zen question about a

CHAPTER 16 - SATSANG WITH MICHAEL

person's face before being born. Michael then said, "The answer is, they haven't got one. There is nobody there. If you want enlightenment, all you have is one monk asking another monk, 'What is the meaning of life?' and the other monk replying, 'Yes.'

Michael repeated the question: "What is your face before you are born?"

Answering himself, he said "I become a nobody to be who I really am. Knocks 'me' out, means enlightened as far as possible. Let yourself sub-let yourself, not being who you appear to be. A 'nobody' is somebody who is empty of self." I'll have to meditate on that, I said. "There is nobody there to meditate," Michael commented.

Michael also talked about being a 'nobody' in another context - because he couldn't get into the film/theatre business. Another remark by Michael, "Give up giving up."

Q: What's it like being a Zen master?
A: "Being drunk."

Q: What's the sound of one hand clapping?
A: "Air."

Q: What is the ego?
A: "What does that mean?" "The problem with duality is that it has two sides. One side too many."

Q: How many sides does awareness or consciousness have?
A: "Non-dual shine."

Astonishingly, this comment perfectly corresponded to the sketch I had been drawing at home that morning, for mirror-surfaced sculptures of the Möbius Band and Klein Bottle.

These are objects which curiously only have one surface, not two. "You go to the top of the class", I said. Michael nonetheless insisted that his comment "non-dual shine" was derived from Sri Ramana Maharshi.

Q: Who are you?
A: "Consciousness shining."

Q: How is your consciousness shining today?
A: "I went into it today."

Q: How is self-remembering today? (This time, Michael gave another enigmatic answer.)
A: "Rain by dawn. I have to work out whether I can catch a cold from the rain, of course."

Q: Can you say something about spiritual isolation?
A: "Ultimately, spiritual isolation has nothing to do with isolation; it has to do with connectedness."

He's talking about the Unity principle here.

CHAPTER 16 - SATSANG WITH MICHAEL

He loves playing with words:

"All-connected-ness, all-one, not alone." Then Michael added ""Alone .... bon; naturally, you don't swallow the bone", he said!

Q: What caused that spiritual crisis?
A: "It's only a game."

Q: How does the game go?
A: Self-study.

Q: What helped you to overcome your spiritual crisis?
A: "Self-remembering. Self-study is Self-Remembering - - it's only a game.", he repeated. "En joue[2]."

Q: Can you answer the question, "Who am I?"
A: Jokingly, he said, "Maharshi"

I recounted my thoughts about when somebody says to me, as I leave them... "Take care." Apart from conventional idiomatic use, that is, often used informally to express good wishes when parting, at the end of a message, etc the negative mind comes in with thoughts like "could they mean take care because I look ill , or old or something?" I like to have a mental add-on to hearing that, which is: 'Take care to remember who you really are".

I showed Michael the email reply I had just sent to my

friend in Malta. I had written that for the last two hours, I had been with Sri Ramana Michael, to which Michael responded, "Okay, fair enough". A comment that Michael commonly makes.

Musing on Buddha's statement about the three marks or stains of existence, about suffering, impermanence and the ego (no-self), as experienced by all sentient beings. These were Michael's answers.

Q: Is the 'I' that is aware of the suffering of all beings also sentient?
A: "Of course."

Q: Is the awareness of no-self also sentient?
A: "If a man and a woman are having a cup of tea and don't add anything there, then there is nothing (added) there."

Q: Is there such a thing as death?
A: "The Clear Light of the Void appears after death. The soul leaves the body."

Q. What about the ego?
A. "What does that mean?"

Whilst sitting in one of our usual spots, in the area of Clapham Junction, on the road called Lavender Hill, I told Michael this story about Sri Ramana Maharshi.

CHAPTER 16 - SATSANG WITH MICHAEL

When he was old, and nearing death, his devotees brought their sickto him on the mountain where he lived in a cave.

They pleaded with him. "Our sick are healing here in your presence. Please don't leave us." "Where is there to go?" said Ramana. Michael then said, "My soul belongs to the void, the clear light of the void". Then I asked, "If your soul belongs to the void, where do you belong?" "This looks like Lavender Hill," Michael answered, grinning broadly. I couldn't stop laughing very loudly. Then after a short pause, "You are always welcome," Michael said grinning again.

In an earlier conversation, Michael had said that his heart belongs to Paris.

Q: Where does your soul belong?
A: "The void... Bardo."

Referring to the tradition about the non-existence or death of the ego, I said that I'd like to die before I die. Michael then said, "The clear light of the void will appear". Discussing Covid, I mentioned that at that time, more than a million were listed as dead, so the void is getting very full. Michael said the void is a Tibetan idea. Bardo, I said he nodded in agreement.

I mentioned that Tibetans believe in reincarnation...

Q: What do you think of reincarnation?
A: "There is no guarantee of it."

Q: The Tibetans are very strong on finding or choosing the next Dalai Lama through the system of reincarnation.
A: As long as they don't choose me!

Q: Have you met anyone else who was a self-realised being?
A: "Gurdjieff."

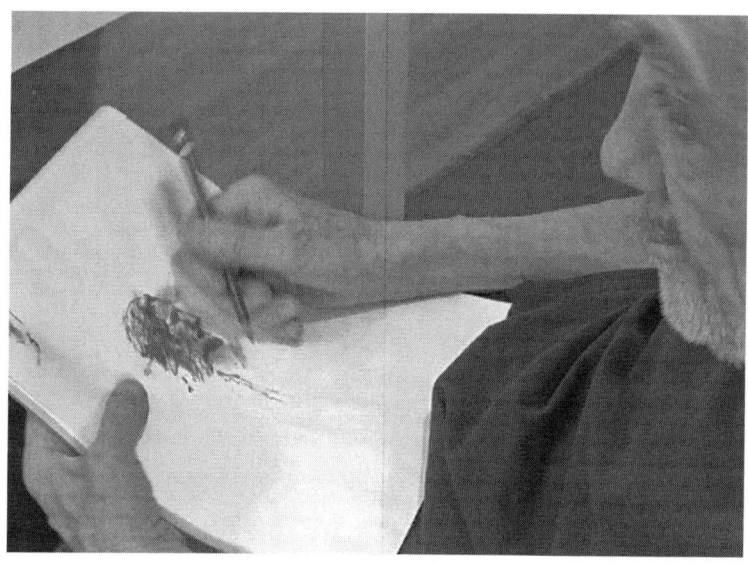

An important lesson was given to me in an unexpected way. I had been encouraging Michael to make a drawing of his father for inclusion in this book. He eventually made one, a copy, from a photograph, in pencil, a small profile which involved a lot of rubbing out. I liked it and was going to photograph it on my next visit to him to use in the book. However, when I looked through his drawing pad, the drawing had disappeared! It seems that Michael had destroyed it. I

CHAPTER 16 - SATSANG WITH MICHAEL

had put a lot of effort into supporting Michael to start making some art and to make this in particular. It had taken quite a few weeks of encouragement, to get Michael to make this drawing. So naturally, I was a bit irked. Luckily, I'd managed to snap a shot of him working on it.

Now here is the learning. A key to this is to understand how attachment to things or outcomes can lead to various degrees of unhappiness when lost. When I learnt that Michael had destroyed that drawing, I had said to him, "That's very naughty of you!" Actually, one could interpret Michael's performance or act, as a slap to my attachment towards the drawing. In other words, a call to wake-up.

Michael is not the first 'sage' to behave like this. Gurdjieff was notorious for unexpectedly and somehow spontaneously `being very naughty. For example, there's an interesting video[3] where Gurdjieff and Ouspensky were taking a train journey, and suddenly out of the blue, Gurdjieff jumps up, pretends to be drunk, becomes very loud and raucous and disturbs the peace of the people sitting in the carriage.

He even poured a drink over a lady passenger nearby. He hadn't touched a drop of alcohol, yet he was bumping and knocking into people as if he was completely inebriated. This performance was indubitably for the benefit of his friend and biographer, who accompanied him on many of his journeys, the much more conservative quiet and predictable academic Ouspensky. I have no idea what Gurdjieff was trying to teach Ouspensky, but certainly,

Ouspensky was very upset by his friend's goings-on. There are many similar stories, with Zen Masters and other spiritual teachers. For example, Osho and Da John could be cited as such, though I wouldn't want to recommend their lifestyles or behaviours.

Perhaps this is all about letting go of our expectations and attachments about how a teacher ought to behave.

From the non-dual perspective, as Michael has often quoted, Ouspensky's writings gleaned from Gurdjieff that 'it's all a game', and these aberrant behaviours point out the folly of taking this dream that we live in too seriously. I am sure this story will cause some controversy amongst our readers.

Michael said, "You can either take drugs, or you can take Ouspensky."

However, there is another insight which occurred to me, as I drove home from that visit, from the above story. Whether or not Michael was providing a 'lesson' for me, which he later denied, or whether he just didn't like the drawing he had created, is not the key to the learning. One has to look the other way, inwards, and see what is going on there.

That is if I am judging this action as deleterious, such that I get annoyed or upset, allowing my inner peace and calmness to evaporate or alternatively, I could see it as an opportunity to practise the art of 'letting go', which invites calm and inner spaciousness.

CHAPTER 16 - SATSANG WITH MICHAEL

This choice of how one may look at any troubling occurrence could be applied across the board to many incidents in our daily lives. Each thus becomes an opportunity to allow ourselves to shine more.

One may similarly consider the story of Gurdjieff related above. Ouspensky once wrote in a book that the transformation of negative emotions is indeed recommended.

Q: What's the best practice for following the Way?
A: "Stop the expression of negative emotions."

Going back to Michael's yoga practice, there was this exercise that Solange showed Michael, holding the arms out horizontally[4]. Solange was the wife of Lubansky; they ran a Fitness First class 40 years ago.

Q: How do you control negative emotions?
A: Raising both arms up in the air for about ten minutes, though definitely not medicine, can still be effective. Holding the arms horizontally for ten minutes is transformational. This is yoga.

Q: What's the secret of happiness?
A: "Health."

Q: What do you mean by Health?
A: "A healthy Mind and a healthy body."

I love what I might call significant synchronicities. Just as we were speaking, a van passed by with the company name emblazoned on its side, 'Sanctuary Maintenance'.

Q: What's a healthy mind?
A: "If you stop expressing negative emotions and give up thoughts, you will never feel the lack of energy. This is health."

Note: It has been estimated that we have, on average, 60,000 to 80,000 thoughts a day! Wow! That must consume a lot of our energy. Do check out my other upcoming books called 'Could Some of Your Thoughts Be Hurting You?' and 'How To Be The Best You Can Be" Look out for these next books on Amazon in 2024.

Q: What's a healthy body?
A: "Don't scratch it."

Michael had been suffering from itching recently. I asked Michael if he managed to avoid scratching. He'd had some medication for it, and I asked whether the ointment did work. "Fair," he replied, then he said, "Feeling and scratching are different things - thinking and knowing are different. That's Important to note."

Michael sometimes suggested health remedies to me. For example, he said that vitamin Z (zinc) is good for immunity, and he also told me that milk thistle was

CHAPTER 16 - SATSANG WITH MICHAEL

recommended for the stomach. Michael then surprisingly came out with this little anecdote from one of his father's 'Proudfooteries'.

"The lighthouse keeper; had a horse; he didn't use it much, of course, but oh! How patiently; the horse waited; for the lighthouse keeper's leave on shore."

Michael had seen this as a neat little 'test' for the egoic mind, or puzzle, like a zen koan.

The lighthouse keeper is a guardian or gatekeeper of the mysterious awakened state. Evidently, patience is required by the embodied soul, possibly represented by the horse. Waiting undemanding, for 'grace' to be given, when the horse and the lighthouse keeper can become One, and gallop off together, taking 'leave' of the state of separation, work, duality, samsara, and enjoy the Oneness of non-dual galloping bliss. That's the real holiday.

Many texts could be unwrapped in this way, when understood rightly, they points to the way 'home'. A classic example is found in Shakespeare's writings which beg to reveal their hidden meaning. "All the world's a stage, and all the men and women merely players," from As You Like It by Shakespeare.

Michael quoted an actor who said... the key to being a successful actor, when it gets dark, people should go to bed and get up when it gets light. There's a deeper

www.moichcreations.com

meaning here too, though Michael rarely articulates it in a mundane way. If you get it, a galloping we will go!

Michael then told me of an event that he'd read about some two or three months earlier regarding criminals dressing up as police and calling on Kim Kardashian, and stealing her stuff. About an hour later, I went and got that day's Evening Standard for Michael, which had just come out, and he immediately pointed out, on the front page, a photo of Kim Kardashian. "Had you seen the newspaper before?" I asked. "No," he said. "You must be psychic", said I. Michael often mentions some topic, says some word or phrase, which is remarkably prescient to the matter in hand.

Q: What advice do you have for young people to have a good life?
A: Connect with people who can assist them with whatever they need.

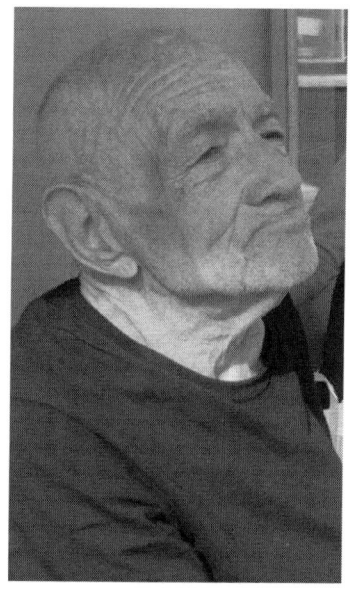

Q: If you had a chance to sit with the Buddha, what question would you ask him?
A: I would ask him if he is in pain.

Michael replied to the following question with a really obscure answer:

CHAPTER 16 - SATSANG WITH MICHAEL

Q: What's it like, being you?
A: The cake is very filling - I like carrot cake, but I don't like being sick, he said while pointing to his catheter.

Q: Is anything interesting in the newspaper you've just read (Evening Standard)?
A: It's me.

Q: In all your years of being on Lavender Hill, what have you achieved?
A: Nil. I make way for others of different intelligence to seek out their salvation.

Q: All these years hanging around here (Battersea), has it achieved what you wanted?
A: Yes, it achieved nothing. Nil.

Q: What is the meaning of your pointing a finger upwards towards the sky (His other hand usually points towards his heart)?
A: Union with God (Brahma)

At the end of the day, as I waffled on about the mating habits of birds, "Give up thoughts!" said Michael. I showed Michael the last page of a book called 'Being Bliss." He summed it up by saying "I've read worse!" Sometimes Michael's remarks have more bizarre content. Michael asked "Where are the dogs? If you ever see a dog walking backwards, what's happening? Self-enquiry." Dog God?

At one point, Michael had mentioned the name of the landlord where his mother used to stay in Richmond, but then he said to me, "Don't mention him; he was not historically important." He followed this up by saying, "You are the most unimportant person I have met, as unimportant as God." A very curious, interesting and enigmatic remark.

Clearly, Michael has a sense of the people in his life who were historically important, and there were many of them. In another strange conversation, Michael said that he had three souls. I asked him to tell me about them. "One of the souls belonged in the void," he said. "It would have stayed there if I hadn't got back," Michael added. "I called to come back." I think he was referring to an incident when he nearly died... a near-death experience?

The other two souls? Michael had spilt curry on the floor and inadvertently stepped on it. The other two soles (souls), were evidently those of his shoes, which he was attempting to clean by walking on tea that he poured on the floor. I quipped about Jesus walking on water - "Michael walking on tea".

He may have stepped in trickles (of urine). Michael then spelt out the name Tickle, a person killed in the first World War. "I read about him in the library," Michael said.

CHAPTER 16 - SATSANG WITH MICHAEL

More tea stories:

"I couldn't make tea where I used to live (Connor Court) - the kettle needs a 'slight' cleaning." Michael pointed to the catheter extension 'bag' on his leg and said it needed emptying.

I observed that he had better eyesight than me, spotting all sorts of interesting things, for example, the Mondrian design on the shopping trolley of a passer-by, or commenting on a series of interesting cars, as they raced up Lavender Hill. Indeed, Michael enjoyed seeing smart, special cars.

This no doubt harks back to the days of being driven about in his father's yellow open top Rolls Royce. In our time together, in the last year or so, it also became obvious to me that Michael had a sharp eye for a pretty girl. With the excuse of commenting, as an artist, on the colour of their dress, he often drew my attention to a passing beauty. "Very healthy," he would add. Michael was then 87. I suggested, jestingly, that he had such good eyesight and vision because of being surrounded by angels in Heaven for so many aeons.

Michael quite often seemed to be talking to himself; he definitely doesn't have a mobile phone or hands-free device to be talking to a real person. I asked Michael about that, and I once asked him whether he was conversing or arguing with someone. Michael clarified that he sometimes argues with himself. I asked him if arguing and negative emotions are bound together. "Oh no!" Michael replied, "However, this time, I was practising 'There's No You' by Frank Sinatra."

Other chats:

Another time, while keeping in mind a hospital appointment that Michael needed to go to the next day, we were talking about what time Michael needed to get up. Michael then digressed into one of his stranger comments. "People don't need to sleep," Michael said. "But they are fictional, of course. I don't want to talk about real people at all, so that's why I call it fictional." I told Michael the story of when I was a teenager and had a holiday job with a printer. I had seen an elderly looking woman attempting to lift and move a pile of packages of paper. So, I offered to help and lifted a pile up to carry them for her.

Suddenly, a male worker rushed up to me and said that I can't do that. "You'd be taking the bread out of our mouths. We have a union here," he said. After telling Michael this story, I said that reference to 'Union' in the anecdote reminds me of Michael telling me, that when he points his finger up to the heavens, it means 'Union with God'.

One time, Michael pointed out a soft-topped car, possibly a Chevrolet. I commented that I did not care for soft-topped cars. "But I do because I don't get sick in an

CHAPTER 16 - SATSANG WITH MICHAEL

open-top car, whereas, I sometimes do in a closed-top one", Michael responded. I said that I could relate to that as I used to get sick when my father took our family to the seaside in a little old Ford car.

Michael has a strange obsession with the police as to whether they could or would accuse him of anything. He once bizarrely said, "The nearer the police are to me, the nearer I am to prison". `This must relate to some unfortunate experience he must have had which got stuck in his mind. He sometimes referred to this concern in what seemed a semi-serious way.

Here's a little anecdote that I'm a bit embarrassed about. Two policemen were approaching, and I inappropriately made a joke, moving a bit further along and away on the bench from Michael, "Policemen are coming. I don't know you." I continued by mentioning Peter (the Apostle) saying something similar about not knowing Jesus. Michael responded, "He got crucified after all". Then Michael calmed everything down with his usual "Give Up thoughts."

From the Non Dual perspective, nothing belongs to me. The illusion of separateness comes from a sense attachment to stuff.

'I' is often not what we think it is.

Pervasive self-awareness, awareness of yourself as a person, personality... I wish that would go away... like clouds, but it doesn't seem to, unless you get this strange perspective.

All is One... I am you... But I don't know what your bank balance is. There is only one question... Who exactly am I? The invitation is to find that me who seeks answers.

Hearing Michael's responses, as we chatted and passed time together, when I could understand them, reminded me of spiritual teachers I have read about such as Ramana Maharishi and Nisargadatta. (Michael looks a little like Nisargadatta in this photo.)

CHAPTER 16 - SATSANG WITH MICHAEL

Footnotes:

1. Satang, "Satsang" is a Sanskrit term that means "association with truth" or "company of the wise." In contemporary terms, it refers to a gathering or community where individuals come together to discuss, explore, and share spiritual or philosophical teachings, often led by a knowledgeable guide or teacher.

2. It's only a game, Michael says, but it would perhaps be better to refer to the drama of life as a play. To call it a game is to belittle the seriousness that the actor commits to playing his part in the drama of life even though the character portrayed is not real. (The part I play is Moich. Is Moich simply a character? If so, who is the actor? Who am I really, then?)

3. See 'Gurdjieff: The Rascal Saint – Sadhguru Exclusive' (YouTube video) https://tinyurl.com/2efwt5xx

4. Michael derived this practice from studying the fakirs, sadhus or yogis from India in the 17th century. They hung themselves upside down for long periods. Others used to roll boulders about. Two disciplines that Michael likes to practise are holding his arm up in the air, or holding his leg off the ground especially holding one or both arms vertically above his head.

CHAPTER 17

The three M's

"Be kind, aim for the Heart."
                              Alexandre Dumas

CHAPTER 17 - THE THREE M'S

This last chapter is about how Michael came to move into his new lovely cosy home. This came about in an unexpected way and was then facilitated by Maddie and me, as the story will explain. It turned out that the move was quite a saga, and involved a lot of phases and organising, and for this, Maddie was a star. Despite working full time, she did an amazing job liaising with the various management teams and social Services, and many practical issues related to the move. Michael said to Maddie, "You are a vehicle of wonderfulness."

I, being retired, had more time than her to spend with Michael, supporting the transition. Maddie came up with the idea of calling the three of us the three Ms, M1, M2 and M3. She said Michael was M1, I was M2, and she was M3 and referred to her and myself as the Dream Team, for supporting Michael as we did.

This is how it began: Michael hadn't turned up for several days at his usual haunts, Greggs, Boots or Jacks in Clapham Junction. So, I took a chance and went to his flat. It was my first visit there, hoping to find out what had happened to him. Hitherto, Michael hadn't allowed me to visit him there because of the state he kept his flat in.

Access to the building turned out to be challenging. It was like trying to enter a vault in Fort Knox. One couldn't enter the building without a pass key. Getting to the door of Michael's flat at Connor Court, where he had lived for more than ten years, proved even more tricky. Michael lived on the third floor but refused to take the lift - he's probably claustrophobic, and also, usually, he can't stand being physically close to people, especially if they are smoking - so he would always walk up the three flights of steps, and sometimes he could barely walk!

The corridor on his floor is also accessed only by means of another pass key, which I didn't possess. At the locked entrance to that corridor, there was an intercom, and I had to use that to get his attention in his flat. However, Michael is very, very deaf, and consequently, one has to be really close to his left ear for him to hear anything; his right ear is almost completely deaf. Luckily, after dialling his flat number repeatedly... I didn't give up... Michael eventually answered the intercom to his flat, and told me in a husky voice..." I am sick and have to stay in bed - see you in a few days," he said. That sounded promising.

However, Michael didn't show up for a further week. So, I went to his flat again, this time with Maddie. She, fortunately, had acquired a spare key to Michael's floor, so we could now get past the door with the intercom, and actually get to his door. We rang his doorbell repeatedly and banged on the door loudly for quite a long time.

Eventually, a very ill-looking Michael, opened it a tiny crack. We could see that he was extremely run down. He'd always been very thin, never eating properly, and now he looked like a skeleton.

CHAPTER 17 - THE THREE M'S

It transpired that he had spent 10 days sick at Connor Court with no food or sleep, and he had become very dehydrated. We immediately called 999, and the wonderful NHS ambulance people promptly came. It later transpired that this brush with a near-death experience was a blessing in disguise.

Though I had often heard Michael describe his flat, on this occasion, I was able to take a peek inside whilst the ambulance paramedics were attending to Michael, as he lay on the floor, in the corridor, outside his flat. This position, on the floor, had been at Maddie's suggestion when he first appeared looking so weak and ill at his door.

So, I saw his flat there, for the first time. Without going into details, his flat had become unfit for living in. Clearly, Michael had not been able to manage to look after the place and also his self-care and hygiene[1]. I don't wish to describe it more, other than to say, his existence in that flat was what one might describe as feral[2].

The two wonderful ambulance paramedics, examined him thoroughly, and they also, one at a time, checked his flat out. When they saw the state of it, they, in fact, took photos of it for their report. Michael was duly taken to Chelsea and Westminster Hospital in Fulham, where he stayed for three weeks. Here, they addressed his kidney infection, malnourishment and general health and at the end of that stay, he was beginning to look healthy again. I did manage to visit him a few times whilst he was there.

Thus, it occurred that after Michael's close encounter or near scrape with death - for my intuition was that if our intervention had not occurred, Michael may indeed well have perished and gone into the 'void', he now was given a new lease of life. After being 'rescued' by the Dream Team, and having spent those weeks as a patient in Chelsea and Westminster hospital, the brilliant Maddie organised for him to go from the hospital to stay in Ashmead Care Home in Putney for a short period.

This was intended as temporary and short care and for a

CHAPTER 17 - THE THREE M'S

'respite' placement until his flat was 'cleaned up' by the Council. However, in the following few weeks, Maddie and I revisited Michael's flat, for Maddie now had been given the key by Michael, who trusted her implicitly. We observed that the cleaning of the flat was only partially done and still left the place, according to Maddie and me, unfit to live in.

The previous year, due to Covid, Maddie had lost her high-powered job in event organising, and had actually worked as a temporary part-time carer in an Assisted Housing Facility called Prince of Wales Drive.

Whilst Maddie worked there, we had the opportunity to take Michael for a visit, for him to check out the place. He had a tinkle on the piano in the lounge, where he also met a couple of residents and even played Scrabble with one of them. However, true to form, at that time, Michael said, "No, No... I'll think about it... I've things to do first", and all sorts of excuses, and the offer of a new flat there, at that time, fell through.

However, Maddie kept contact with them and hence was in a great position to know about apartment availability.

She researched, via those contacts, and ascertained that they did have vacancies again, at this time. She spoke to the management to ask if Michael could re-apply for a flat - all of which helped to speed things up. Then she successfully liaised with Social Services, for them to help expedite the request.

Thus with great resourcefulness, she began to organise for

Michael the 'possibility' of Michael moving from Connor Court to a new home in this great place which offered independent living with assisted care.

With Michael's near-death experience added into the equation for us to work with, the Dream Team began diplomatically persuading Michael that this was the time to accept a move. I actually argued, that since he loved feeding his precious pigeons and crows, if he went back to his old flat, he would indubitably get sick again and die, and, therefore wouldn't be able to carry on feeding them. So, in order to do that, he best makes efforts to stay alive.

Michael's attitude to change was always like being a stick in the mud. It may sound naïve and implausible, but with his recent experience of being very, very ill, my argument did help Michael to think differently now. "Sweet the uses of adversity," from the play A Midsummer Night's Dream, by Shakespeare. Michael getting sick led to Michael having the opportunity to having a better time for his remaining embodied days.

Whilst at the 'Respite Home' Ashmead, for those several weeks, Michael had gotten used to sleeping in a warm environment with a clean bed, and having people look after him.

To cut a long story short, miraculously, Michael changed his mind this time and accepted moving. The penny must have finally dropped, and Michael now agreed to

CHAPTER 17 - THE THREE M'S

the idea and was willing to accept being rehoused.

This was inNovember 2020.

Paperwork takes ages in these matters, and the date of moving from Ashmead to Prince of Wales Drive kept being postponed. So, time and again, Michael was granted further leave to remain in the 'respite' care home. This was also partly due to the fact that Covid was rife in London, and extra care needed to be taken with elderly people. This also meant that at that time, it was not encouraged to visit care homes because of the pandemic causing so many deaths amongst the elderly in them. In fact, I didn't visit him at all whilst he was there, just a few phone calls. Maddie did manage a few visits as his unofficial voluntary carer, meeting him in a hut they provided on the premises, specially designed for one-to-one visits, with a big plastic or glass barrier between them. He had his first Covid inoculation jab in Ashmead. Ultimately, Michael stayed in Ashmead Care Home for three months!

We had been on tenterhooks waiting to see if he might change his mind and renege on his decision to move and whether he would actually sign the tenancy agreement. The offer was obviously dependent on Michael doing this. We were told that as part of the deal, Michael would have at least 10 hours a week of in-house support. This included two visits a day to see how he was, perhaps offering to microwave some food for him - as he has no idea how to use anything technical - and having his bedding changed once a week. This all sounded brilliant to help Michael look after himself better.

So, Maddie and I had waited nervously to see whether he would actually sign the tenancy agreement, which he finally did, with the help of the manager at the respite carehome, and a lovely social worker. Ultimately, all this was achieved. Hoorah! Michael moved to his new home on the 1st of February, 2021.

Michael's new place is in one of the wings of Creative Support - Prince of Wales Drive Extra Care Service and is called Mary Court. Maddie took on the task of furnished Michael's flat to be, as it was empty, prior to him moving in. Michael had given her his bank card so she was able to go shopping, and she did an excellent job.

The settling in period

The management talked about a six-week period for settling in, after which Social Services would review Michael's needs and how the support is working for him. During Michael's first four weeks, I visited him daily, as his 'bubble' person. This greatly supported his acclimatising to his new environment.

When discussing laundry (in his new apartment). Michael told me, showing it with some physical gestures, how pigeons self-groom. "I can learn about cleanliness from the pigeons," he said, "and can pay them with nutrition" (feeding them bread from his lunch sandwich, as he likes to do).

CHAPTER 17 - THE THREE M'S

One of Michael's main mantras, particularly when asked about doing something different. "I'll think about it." I noticed that sometimes when demands were made of him by his new carers regarding, for example, what he should wear at night, he sometimes displayed somewhat of a temper. Even a tantrum, one could say. Later, perhaps more for his own self-reflection, Michael quoted Ouspensky as saying, "You must not let yourself get into a bad temper."

I was able to see how the carers operated and offered my experience, knowing Michael as well as I do, with tips as to how they could best support him. Some appreciated that, but others may not have. Michael, in his new assisted independent living apartment, had three visits a day from his new carers. One of them, late in the evening, assists Michael to put his pyjama top on as a first step to preparing him for bed - something he didn't use to do before.

The embodied Michael can be very stubborn about any change to his habitual behaviours. Michael responded, "I'm dead myself. In principle, I am dead, and humility is key." This is where Michael and I had an enlightening conversation about his ideas regarding his philosophy, as recorded in Chapter 10.

Another interesting conversation started with Michael saying, "I am a sphinx." I replied, "You are definitely a sphinx," To which he said, "Thank you." He then asked, "Why did one of the carers give me five pills but then took two back?" and I responded, "Nobody is perfect." Michael then added, "I make nothing but mistakes. I am near mistakes the whole time. Thinking, speaking and writing. So, I can't blame someone interested in Macbeth.". Another bizarre reference.

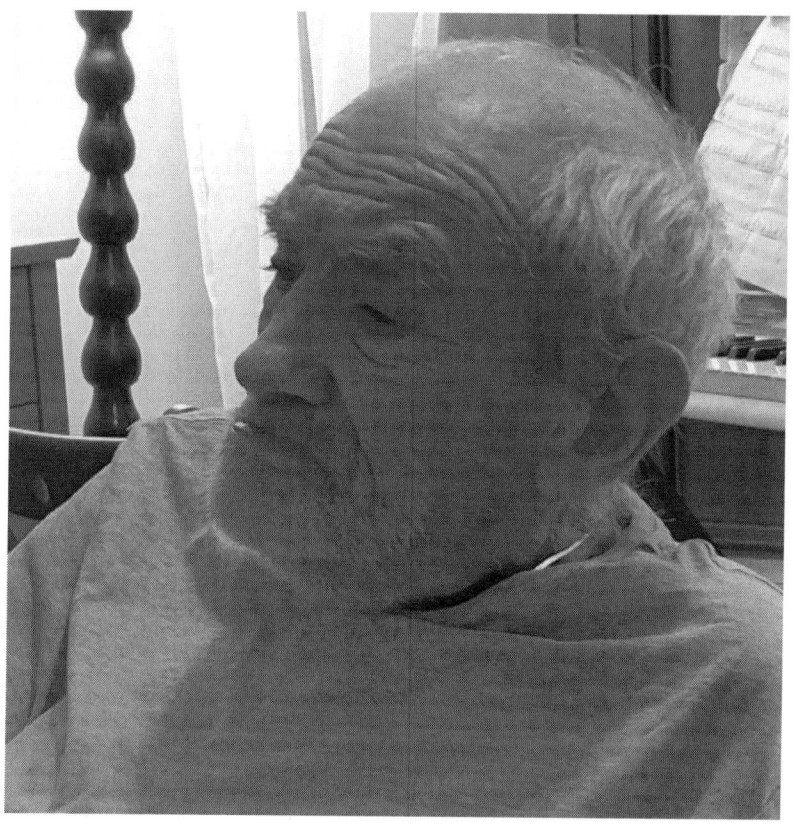

He resumed his afternoon visits to Clapham Junction and over all seems very content in his new home. (Seen as in the photo above.)

Not long after moving into his new apartment, during the

CHAPTER 17 - THE THREE M'S

evening, one of the carers commented to Michael whilst assisting him putting his upper pyjamas on, that Michael had a very good sense of balance.

The very next day, on one of his first venturings out to Clapham Junction again, on his return, as he was coming to his No. 344 bus home, on the edge of the kerb stop in Clapham Junction, very near the bus stop, in Falcon Road, Michael missed his footing and fell!

I explained to Michael that when I tripped and fell, last year, I broke my nose. So, he was lucky that nothing was broken. The last thing he needed at his age was to go into hospital with something broken. Michael recalled the incident when he was at Cheltenham School when a fellow pupil had punched him on the nose breaking it. I then told Michael that something similar had happened to me.

When I was about fifteen in my grammar school, this chap who was a star athlete, didn't like me chatting to a girl in the class that he fancied. We were walking together after school in the direction of the town, and suddenly, he slammed his fist sideways into my nose, which became very bloody. At that time, this chap seemed larger than life physically, to us average kids.

However, curiously, 60 years later, we met up at a grammar school reunion for our class. Now he no longer looked like a giant compared to me but rather the opposite, and indeed, we recalled the incident; he also remembered that he had a guilty conscience for years over this event, and he apologised to me.

Describing what happened to Michael at the bus stop in Clapham Junction at the time, it was clear and obvious that he had fallen badly, pole axed, cutting his upper forehead quite seriously. Michael said there was only a small amount of blood poured onto the pavement, but he had a nasty gash on his forehead, a couple of centimetres above his 'third eye'. It's a very busy bus stop, and some kind people came to his assistance. He grabbed one gentleman's ankle and leg and was helped up. After resting on the sidewalk, he eventually managed to get on his bus and returned back home to his new assisted housing residence. One of the carers took a look. Then Michael went to his apartment flat, and cleaned up the wound himself. It did look like a very nasty bloody scab - an inch wide and three or four inches above his eyebrows. He commented, "it doesn't make me Lord Krishna, just an ordinary idiotic pedestrian." Indian Hindus mark that place on the forehead where consciousness is. Michael said humans are poor devils.

In his new home, Michael loves to practise on his new piano keyboard, which replaced the one in his previous residence, which was deemed to be unsuitable for rescuing. He also loves to spend time doing his 'yoga', and he likes me playing a few of his favourite tunes and songs on the little speaker device, reading the papers, doing the Metro crossword puzzles

CHAPTER 17 - THE THREE M'S

and reading his favourite books, like Moliere in French.

He absolutely loves when Maddie visits him, sometimes taking him shopping. One special visit was on Michael's 87th birthday, and as seen in the picture, Maddie lent Michael her hat. He looked really cool.

Also, of course, Michael enjoys having little spiritual non- dual exchanges with me. Life looks so much better from now on. Although, as Michael says "It's only a game", it looks like his new environment, will now be a much more pleasant one for Michael to play his part in.

Michael is creature of habit, and in this cosy apartment, as time went on, Michael seems happier to stay safe and spend much more time there. His visits to the town centre became less and he was not very often to be seen in his usual haunts. Perhaps his days of hanging out in the streets of Clapham Junction and Lavender Hill may be over. He was 90 in May 2023.

Footnotes:

1. Sri Ramana Maharshi sitting in filth in the early days of 'enlightenment' although Michael probably continued not taking care of himself because of his embodied[2] personal issues. Actually, many people who have a profound 'spiritual awakening', as in the non-dual sense, wherein the ego has lost its grip on what is going on, have a period of being out of touch with mundane existence.

CHAPTER 17 - THE THREE M'S

2. Another famous modern example of this is how Eckhart Tolle sat for a couple of years on park benches in Russell Square, London. He stayed with friends in a Buddhist monastery or otherwise slept rough in Hampstead Heath Park, London, before becoming a world-famous spiritual teacher. Another great example is that of how the Buddha lived prior to his 'Enlightenment', sitting under the Bodhi Tree, absorbed in his meditation, paying no attention to looking after his physical needs.

Postscript

"First there is a book, then there is no book, then there is"
Moich Abrahams, June 2022

"Your own Self-Realization is the greatest service you can render the world."
Ramana Maharshi

Thank you for reading this book! For vibrant, full-color photos by Michael, in-depth discussions on the Direct Path, and a treasure trove of valuable resources, simply visit our upcoming new website at www.moichcreations.com. Explore all we have to offer by clicking the link in your web browser.

There's also an opportunity to receive coaching from Moich Abrahams. Please enquire if interested. You can reach me directly at m@moichabrahams.co.uk

To top it all, at www.moichcreations.com you'll gain access there to see the paintings, prints, and art of the author Moich Abrahams for you to enjoy.

Printed in Great Britain
by Amazon